Praise for
YOUR RADICAL LIVING CHALLENGE

"In her wonderfully wild book, Battista takes us on two road trips: one that spans across America and one that drives us into the peculiar world of the human heart."

— **Joshua Mohr,** author of *Damascus*

"Marni's *Your Radical Living Challenge* offers a bold and refreshing path to designing a life of true meaning—one grounded in spiritual principles and real-life action steps. A must-read!"

— **Mary Morrissey**, founder of Brave Thinking Institute and creator of the DreamBuilder Program

"Using her own cross-country adventures in an RV as inspiration, Marni Battista takes the reader on a rousing journey of self-discovery. *Your Radical Living Challenge* is a provocative and motivating guide to finding—and staying on—a true course. It's a game-changer for anyone seeking to revamp their relationship with the essential self."

— **Terri Cheney**, *New York Times* best-selling author of *Manic: A Memoir*

"Marni Battista is an agent of change and a beacon of light in the world. *Your Radical Living Challenge* welcomes readers along for the ride on her life redesign while guiding us through conceptualizing our own. The seven spiritual questions and Battista's outlook break from the typical binary 'good/bad outcomes' thought process, illustrating how life can be experienced as a series of fun and fascinating experiments instead."

— **Shawna Kenney**, author of *I Was a Teenage Dominatrix*

"Everyone's journey is amazing; Marni's more so than most. You will wish for her courage, and she will show you how to find it."

— **Steve Leder**, *New York Times* best-selling author

"Enough already! It's time to break free from societal norms and redefine success on your terms. In *Your Radical Living Challenge,* Marni Battista shows you how to move beyond the 'white picket fence' ideals and start living with true meaning and joy. Having spent 20+ years helping others shed expectations and embrace their authentic selves, I can say that this book offers both aspirational insights and practical tools to help you build a fulfilling life from the inside out."

— **D. Luke Iorio,** partner, Man on Fire and
former president and CEO of iPEC

"One thing I've learned from interviewing successful people is that they 'say yes first, figure it out later.' *Your Radical Living Challenge* empowers you to do just that—discover the things that make you feel most alive and say yes to them. Marni's book guides you to deconstruct and reconnect with the version of yourself that is happiest, most grateful, and most fully you. Start living the life you deserve!"

— **Michael O'Neal,** host of *The Solopreneur Hour*

YOUR

RADICAL
LIVING

CHALLENGE

YOUR
RADICAL
LIVING
CHALLENGE

7 Questions for Leading
a Meaningful Life

MARNI BATTISTA

HAY HOUSE LLC
Carlsbad, California • New York City
London • Sydney • New Delhi

Copyright © 2025 by Marni Battista

Published in the United States by: Hay House LLC: www.hayhouse.com®
Published in Australia by: Hay House Australia Publishing Pty Ltd: www.hayhouse.com.au
Published in the United Kingdom by: Hay House UK Ltd: www.hayhouse.co.uk
Published in India by: Hay House Publishers (India) Pvt Ltd: www.hayhouse.co.in

Cover design Shubhani Sakar
Interior design: Bryn Starr Best

The author of this book does not dispense medical advice or prescribe the use of any technique as a form of treatment for physical, emotional, or medical problems without the advice of a physician, either directly or indirectly. The intent of the author is only to offer information of a general nature to help you in your quest for emotional, physical, and spiritual well-being. In the event you use any of the information in this book for yourself, the author and the publisher assume no responsibility for your actions.

Cataloging-in-Publication Data is on file at the Library of Congress

Tradepaper ISBN: 978-1-4019-7618-7
E-book ISBN: 978-1-4019-7619-4
Audiobook ISBN: 978-1-4019-7620-0

10 9 8 7 6 5 4 3 2 1
1st edition, February 2025

Printed in the United States of America

This product uses responsibly sourced papers and/or recycled materials. For more information, see www.hayhouse.com.

*For Max and Jennie,
my great-grandparents who did a radical thing
by leaving Russia to come to America in 1894.*

CONTENTS

AUTHOR'S NOTE

The journey you are about to embark on is the story of my reinvention at 54 years old, as well as a journey into your own self-limiting beliefs and the steps you can take, as I did, to reinvent your life at any age, stage, or phase in life.

We have all been working hard. Achieving. Striving. Yet many of us feel an emptiness inside once we achieve what it is we think was supposed to make us happy or fulfilled. All that BS about "progress rather than perfection" feels like it applies to everyone except us. And when we don't feel happy or content or fulfilled after doing what we thought we should or had to do, we keep searching. We use the same tried-and-true methods for years without experiencing a sense of peace, until one day, we take that last breath, hoping the cross-your-fingers approach to creating a meaningful life was effective.

And so, we spend most of the years of our life ticking boxes off the lists we have of milestones and accomplishments we believe we must achieve to be happy. Jobs to get and money to make and save. Trips to take. Instagram selfies and endless feelings of what psychologists are calling "compare and despair," rather than joy. Perform at the highest level and hope to get rewarded. Yet what really happens is that our esteem becomes increasingly dependent on achieving more and more. Then, when we don't or even if we do, a sense of happiness and fulfillment and meaning remains elusive. We beat ourselves up. Maybe even push harder. Ever striving and never satisfied.

And then, we die.

The solution to all this striving for success is not about filling up time with distractions or putting a Band-Aid over the things in your life that you are tolerating. Or waiting for some elusive "when": when we retire, lose weight, or meet the guy.

Instead, it's about getting radical.

rad·i·cal
/ˈradək(ə)l/
relating to or affecting the fundamental nature of something;
far-reaching or thorough

Your Radical Living Challenge is designed to empower readers to go on a ME journey to create *meaning* from the deepest place of divine authenticity.

While this story involves me selling my house and leaving Los Angeles after 25 years while facing the cracks in my marriage, for you this book might be about not settling for a career you don't love, beginning to date again, overcoming your fear of starting a side hustle, or the need to stop living life on the sidelines once and for all. My story isn't prescriptive in itself. Your journey through these pages and version of success will be unique to you, as that is the point of this book, after all. So, to be sure, your Radical Living Challenge may not look like mine. That said, the process I followed and the seven spiritual questions I teach are universal.

I tested this journey with clients during the two years I worked on writing this book, and here are a few tips they asked me to share with you.

- This book is designed to be a guide to take you through a specific process that will allow you to course correct at any stage of your life. The objective is that you will redefine what success looks like for you. As it is a process, my clients and I recommend you go through each chapter, in order, with a journal and pen nearby to help you reflect on the exercises to guide you in your journey. Readers also suggested that once you get through a chapter, it may be helpful to go back to earlier exercises and chapters as you feel is necessary along the way. Some of the questions are more complex and require more chapters and thus more exercises to master, while others do not. The bottom line: don't skip ahead, but feel free to look in the rearview mirror occasionally and revisit the materials as many times as you need. You may, in fact, want to read the book first and skip the exercises entirely. That too is okay. My vision for you is that this book becomes tattered and torn as you reflect and experiment, reviewing the questions and the exercises over and over again in your lifetime, just as I have over the last eight years or so.

- Certain concepts may not land initially, and that is okay. Keep going. For now, you are a journeyer and a creator. The material in this book is deep, and like a good Bolognese, sometimes things need to simmer a while. Again, keep walking forward. Reflect. Go backward and revisit something. Go slow to get there fast.

- Some tools or exercises I suggest may be perfect for you; others may not feel aligned. The point is to create your personal toolbox and choose what works best for you.

The Seven Questions I share here are not necessarily linear and have been adapted from the original questions as they appeared in the ancient texts from which they came. Rather, because they are spiritual principles, you will find that as you begin to study and adopt them into your life, they will ultimately become the pathway for a more joyful and meaningful way of living life in times of both chaos and joy.

And last, the actual road trip my husband and I took in our RV named Andi serves as a metaphor for the understanding that life is, in fact, a journey. So is the experience of preparing for and being in transition, the process of grief and loss, and all things that happen repeatedly if we are lucky enough to live another day. It is my hope that this book allows you to celebrate all of it and to truly live life so that life merely stops living you.

PROLOGUE

There I was, standing on the precipice of pure exhilaration. Wild, free, and 6,000 feet of elevation between me and my destination. A singular moment of joy in February 2020.

I leaned forward—bent knees, cheeks flushed—my friend's neon-orange ski jacket was just ahead, beckoning me to follow down the steep ski slope. I pushed forward, attacking the terrain. I pushed my way between the moguls, twisting and flying through those oversized cupcakes. I gulped in the crisp stillness of the frigid mountain air, the snowflakes falling onto me, melting into me. The muscles of my legs screamed in ecstasy.

Then, in an instant, I became a body unfurling.

I was falling.

The cacophony of what must have been the edge of my left ski scraping against the ice, scraping, scraping, and my right ski, slicing through the air, awakened me to the understanding that I could not stop or slow myself down.

I was airborne.

Flying.

Falling.

And then, *thwack*!

My back hit the cold Canadian mountaintop with a thud, landing me in a patch of packed snow in the middle of the slope. I lay on my back, my knees bent as if I was ready to do a sit-up, my hands still holding tightly onto the poles resting at my side, as if I might just stand up from there and then carry on traversing down the mountain.

Intuitively I knew I was not able to, though, so I took two deep breaths, confused.

The pain in my back was a dull ache, and so I decided to rest for a minute. I heard my friend yelling my name from the base of the run, asking if I was okay. I raised my gloved hand, still attached to the ski pole, lifting it, signaling to her I was okay but that I could not respond. I had not yet caught my breath.

I half-opened one eye to see an outstretched hand in front of me. A man's hand, offering to help me up.

"No," I said. "Thank you, though. Not yet." I shook my head for emphasis.

"Are you sure?" he asked. "Just grab my hand."

I knew I was not ready to move and realized my eyes were still closed, which is when I realized I could not move, even if I had wanted to, and so, as I heard him ski away, I tried to wiggle my toes deep inside my still-warm, new ski boots.

My plan was to plant my poles uphill when I got to a good spot and lift myself up. But my legs buckled, the pain excruciating, terrifying.

I could not stand.

I knew I would not be skiing the rest of the way down this mountain.

This is the moment my life changed.

Nothing would be the same.

I had broken my back.

Wrapped up in blankets like a burrito, I was skied down the mountain by a patrolman. I was grateful I could feel my feet, even though they were numb with cold. I closed my eyes for a moment and connected to my breath, a deep knowing inside me making itself known. I would somehow be okay. I opened my eyes, listening to the whoosh of the toboggan going down, down, taking in the beauty and even the silliness of the incredible point of view I now had from this unusual vantage point: the vast gray sky and the incredibly tall pine trees sagging under the weight of new fallen snow.

I did not know that moment and the fracturing of my sacrum was the beginning of a journey that would ultimately birth the Radical Living Challenge. That the moment being skied down the hill would lead to this journey of putting myself back together.

INTRODUCTION

Maybe you picked up this book because you are ready to design the last chapter of your life and want it to be magical and full. Maybe you have a vision of starting a location-independent business that will give you the freedom and income to travel. Or maybe you just want to live your life uncaged, wild, and free.

When my dad had died three years before my skiing accident, in the final hours of his life, he had been mumbling something I couldn't understand exactly. But what I do know is that he was trying to sort out something in his mind about credit cards. In that moment at the hospital, I wondered: Does it all *really* come down to credit cards and investment accounts and the kind of car you drive? Eight months later, during a sermon I heard while sitting in a synagogue during the Jewish High Holy Days, the answer to the question I had asked myself in the hospital began to crystallize. In the sermon, I heard a story in which the Talmudic sages of old, in order to determine whether we have lived a meaningful life, ask Seven Questions at the gates of heaven. Five of the questions came from one rabbi, one from another, and the last question from a third. The dogma is that you could then use these questions during your lifetime as a guide to help shape the decisions you make, the values you hope to live by and teach your children, and the strategies you want to utilize to determine your priorities to live a meaningful life.

The questions are essentially this:

- Did you seek wisdom?
- Were you YOU?
- Were you radically honest with yourself?
- Did you busy yourself with creation?
- Did you make time for your spiritual life?

- Were you hopeful?
- Did you recognize the blessing?

At the time I was writing a memoir about my father's life and death, and I began to wonder, had my dad lived a meaningful life according to these seven spiritual questions?

And then I wondered further: Would I?

Digging into the Questions

For the purpose of the work we will do here, I have universalized these questions, expanding and phrasing them in less traditional ways, and changing the order in which they traditionally appear.

When I discovered the seven spiritual questions used throughout this book, it was against the backdrop of significant life events: the loss of my father, the ski accident with an uncertain recovery, an empty nest, and a marriage that sometimes felt like I was living on the San Andreas fault, constantly waiting for the big one that might end it all. I wanted change, yet I was terrified. I believed if I were to find the missing pieces of the puzzle, change might ultimately undermine what I believed was my security and stability.

Can you relate? It's a tricky spot to be in when your fear is as strong as the desire to want more.

So, as you can imagine, deciding to move into 400 square feet with my husband and our cats and our imperfect marriage, selling our house and most of our belongings, and then traveling across America in an RV did not happen overnight. In fact, the entire process from start to end evolved over a period of almost eight years. And I decided to write this book because I do not want you to wait eight years to live *your* meaningful life.

But we will get back to that part shortly.

First, you need to understand who I am.

After divorcing my first husband after 17 years of marriage, I spent five years as a single mom in Los Angeles, living in my LA home, holding down three part-time jobs at once to make a measly 24k a year while commuting to graduate school at night. I hoped

I could go back to work to supplement the temporary alimony I had agreed to receive to provide a lifestyle for my three daughters that would mimic the one they had with their dad, a pharmaceutical tech executive. Shortly before meeting my second husband, though, I had an idea to write a book about my dating misadventures, a topic that I had been fascinated with since a boy in eighth grade asked me to dance and then smirked as he took my chair for himself when I stood up to join him for a dance.

The book idea morphed into getting a loan to obtain a professional coaching certification and start a business helping successful women learn how to date and have healthy relationships. I met my husband, Jeremy, shortly before I held my first professional workshop—an event that went so poorly, half the attendees left before the first break. But over the next 13 years, I was able to turn that business into a venture worth over a million dollars a year with a team of experts and working with clients across the globe.

I had gone from being over $100,000 in debt after my divorce and making 24k a year to finally having a little over a million dollars in savings in a decade. Jeremy and I married in 2014, the same year my alimony ended. I finally had what I worked so hard for. Financial security. A home I loved and had made mine. A new husband and a blended family with our three daughters who were now young adults, whom I had managed to not fuck up along the way. The view of an apple tree I had from my kitchen window where I made coffee each morning felt like the ultimate win.

I didn't want to be self-critical or ask questions.

I was too terrified.

Life felt like a game of Jenga, and I believed that if I were to pull out even one piece, the entire world I had built that had given me a sense of control and security would fall. That is until the traumatic spine injury doctor declared 14 weeks after my ski accident that my sacrum had "healed perfectly." That would have been fantastic news *if I weren't still in chronic pain* nearly six months after my accident. Despite the doctor looking me in the eyes, his dazzling smile a temporary distraction, I was far from healed.

So, let's use my cracked sacrum as a metaphor of what life looked like for me being in that stuck place of both longing for something more meaningful and the feeling of terror I had toward change.

Maybe you will relate.

After that visit to the doctor, the world was in various forms of lockdown, and I navigated through the pain. In my kitchen. In and out of shops, the pain pulsing through my body like the relentless beat of a drum. With each tentative shuffle, my body protested, muscles tense and rigid, as if each movement was a battle against an invisible force. Despite the discomfort, I pressed on, driven by a stubborn resolve to push through the pain, even as my body screamed for respite. Instead, I spent hours Googling questions like "how to heal chronic back pain." I visited doctors and gurus and physical therapists in Los Angeles and even bought an online program that promised miracles once ads promising a cure started to populate my social media feed.

However, nothing changed.

One night, while lying in bed covered in ice packs, I knew I was avoiding not only the extent of the physical pain but also the sadness and the fear that motherhood as I had known it was complete. That I was middle-aged. The repetitive arguments I kept having with my husband. The crushing weight of having to make payroll, knowing that I had not paid myself in months.

Just like the bones the doctor said had healed, the life you have in which everything you've worked for can look good on the outside. But despite looking good, pain still exists. You just don't want to acknowledge the depth of it. Or feel it. Or deal with it. Because you don't know the pathway to healing and joy.

And so, while the seven fractures in my sacrum were technically healed and all the things about my own life looked amazing on the outside, something inside was most definitely off.

Part of my resistance to confronting the pain was that my family, the house we lived in, the work, and the community I had built around me—all the external parts of my life—made me feel safe and in control. While I had the handsome husband to feature on my website and a lovely house and amazing adult children, what was missing was a sense of peace and contentedness inside me. That felt unconditional. I wanted to live a life that had no limits or bounds. I wanted to feel happiness as a sense of aliveness inside me. To know I was living life rather than waiting for it to happen. To feel challenged. Awake. And most of all what I *really* wanted was to stop being afraid of *everything crashing* and to live my life on purpose so that I could make an impact and stop compromising who and what I really was on the inside.

However, like you, I wanted to do it in a way that would feel safe and in control.

So, the question then becomes how do you create freedom when your brain wants to say, "Fuck that"? How do we ponder change, live life on our terms, and still create a feeling of safety? This is the invitation. I did not do this alone, and neither will you since you are here. Because what I know is that the journey will remind you repeatedly that you cannot simply think your way out of your thoughts. You cannot read the label from inside the jar, as they say. It requires tapping into the part that is there if you look and seek wisdom. It also requires honesty—with yourself and others.

But know this: as you begin to live life in alignment with the Seven Spiritual Questions you are about to learn in the pages of this book, you will feel empowered to make better choices throughout your life. You will begin to label what you used to call *mistakes* as *growth opportunities*. You will be able to feel feelings and let them sink in. And the process itself will begin to fill your heart with much more than happiness. It will fill you with a sense of meaning and fulfillment.

I developed a process and a structure to help me with this journey. And that is what I am going to share with you as we continue together. Because like you, I didn't want this journey in Radical Living to feel like I was blowing up my life. So it is with this intention that together we will break the process down into a framework you can apply to your life now as you begin creating what will become your Radical Living Challenge.

The seven cracks in my sacrum reflected the cracks in the foundation upon which I had built my life. It was clear the accident and the months afterward had finally forced me to be quiet enough to listen. What's more, the Seven Questions became the antidote. I had been moving through life like a hummingbird and hadn't even realized it.

I had to break in order to rebuild.

This book is structured to help you do the same. The questions guide our sections with greater exploration of each. Chapters pertaining to each question share my personal journey, followed by action-oriented exercises called Radical Living Challenges. The quotes within the boxes at the end of each are sayings my clients have become familiar with, as I have repeated these takeaways over the years. Post them by your desk, on your wall, or in your heart, as needed.

Question 1

01   Did You Seek Wisdom?

This question asks us if we have developed the ability to be critical and self-critical in a loving and self-compassionate way. Do we ask questions about the experience we have in our lives in a way that can unlock the capacity we have for wisdom? Do we seek better understanding? Do we seek mutual understanding? Do we see the impact of even our smallest actions and to understand the cumulative impact of those actions so that we can make better choices throughout life?

Introduction to Question 1

For the purposes of our work here, I have universalized the Seven Questions, expanded them, and phrased them in less traditional ways as well as changed the order in which they traditionally appear.

That being said, if I reverse engineer how I ended up sitting in the passenger seat of the RV, it all began with the first spiritual question that I asked myself when it was clear that my spine doctor did not have the answer to the questions I asked him again and again. Questions like: Why am I still in pain? Why is this happening to me? And when it was clear the old way of just pushing through to make things better was not going to work, I finally surrendered. And that led me to the first spiritual question. The question that challenges us to seek wisdom.

The first part of this question asks if we are willing. Let me be clear. Your willingness is something that must last beyond the day that you made the decision to live life on your own terms. Take, for example, the day you bought this book. You wanted a change. And in that willingness, you decided to live a meaningful life. While that's amazing, my job is to tell you the truth. And the truth is that your willingness must extend beyond that initial desire into the land of inconvenience, fear, and discomfort. Being willing for the duration requires you to be committed.

When I am at the beginning of walking this journey with clients, they often ask things like: How long will it take to do this? How many hours of work will there be per week? You get the point. My response is simple. If you are anything like me, when you want something, you do whatever it takes to achieve it. Think about your career. College, if you went. Trade school. Building a house. Making a family. All the things you had to do to get where you are in life. If you wanted it, you did what it took. Period. When you think about living life on your terms, it's not about the way; it's about choosing to commit to yourself and making the most of your one very precious life. Again, even when it is inconvenient.

There are two important things to note about this question. First, this question will begin the journey toward a life of meaning and fulfillment and has nothing to do with your career or your bank account. Furthermore, it does not ask if you achieved a certain level of success. And while most of us are raised with a mindset in which approval and even love is won through performing well, this question does not care whether you do, or you do not.

Second, it's important to also recognize that this question is also not asking if you are smart. Or if you are logical or have access to information. Nor does it ask whether or not you have intellectual prowess. Or even whether you know how to problem solve or think critically. It does not ask if we have answers. Instead, the question is asking you to seek wisdom.

Question 1 asks us to be critical in a self-compassionate way. So, let's go back in time to the moment I walked out of the doctor's office that day when he declared my body "healed" and decided to surrender and start asking different questions. You see, I had been lying to myself.

Yes, I had followed the rules, confining myself to bed for the nine weeks it had been prescribed after my diagnosis. And then I had been doing what the physical therapist had instructed me to do during the pandemic-mandated virtual sessions. However, what

I wasn't admitting to myself, let alone anyone else, was that the instant I had started to feel better, I had been jumping on the exercise bike, sneaking in a little extra fifteen minutes here and there to do an online yoga workout. Perform, perform, perform. *If I can't do anything, then no one will love me.* In short, I had been taking on too much and writing it off as another one of my massive accomplishments in overcoming the odds.

So, I found myself unable to walk down the length of my driveway without experiencing massive pain and asking questions like, "Why is this happening to me? Will I ever be able to take a walk my neighborhood again? Why isn't the doctor helping me anymore?" I wasn't asking the kinds of questions that could unlock the wisdom I had inside me. I wasn't seeking a better or deeper understanding of why I had minimized the fact that I had broken my sacrum in several places. Or why I felt the compulsion to be a superstar. I hadn't been willing to see the impact of even my smallest actions and to understand the cumulative impact of those actions from the 60,000-foot view so that I could start to make better choices and reset my life in a different way.

It was clear the accident had finally forced me to be quiet enough to listen. What's more, I knew then that the Seven Questions were the antidote.

CHAPTER 1

Tell Me the Truth
and I'll Show You the Lie

Los Angeles, California

Let's rewind to that pivotal moment I described earlier: there I lay in bed, ice packs pressed against my body, the weight of realization crashing over me. I had to surrender and dare to ask myself the profound questions that would set me on the path to true healing, beginning with the first spiritual question, which asks if you have developed the ability to be critical and self-critical in a loving and self-compassionate way.

I was finally ready to seek wisdom to discover what the accident and my relapse were trying to teach me, and so I became willing to listen for the answers to what was in the way of my recovery in new ways.

During a conversation with a colleague a few weeks later, he casually suggested I had been relying on my physical energy and external conditions to create results in my life.

"You keep moving," he said. "Creating new things, always on the move, as if the motion itself is the source of your happiness." He went on, asking me if I had been listening to what he described as the emotional parts of myself.

Can you relate?

I was struck by this because while I had been meditating and affirming and doing everything I could to deal with the accident and the aftermath, I was still not really stopping to feel and use that emotional intelligence as a basis on which to build my life. The next day, the wisdom burst to the surface in between texting a friend and deciding what to have for dinner. The seven cracks in my sacrum were a reflection of the cracks in the foundation on which I had built my life. When I turned to the Seven Questions, I felt relief wash over me, as if I was a kid sitting with a wise adult who had given me a good reason to not do something inherently bad for me. I had been moving through life like a hummingbird and hadn't even realized it until I listened to the inner wisdom that put it all into focus.

I now knew it was time to make a different structure for my life, to start paying attention to what I love and how I feel, and to use these things to start creating the real cornerstone of who I am rather than just relying on busy-ness and productivity. I had broken my sacrum, the center point, and it was time to identify and truly recognize the Essence of what I am and then use that to find my true direction toward a meaningful life. And so it is from that point that I followed the steps I will outline in this book.

Hitting the Road

Nearly 24 months exactly from the moment I was skied down the mountain by the ski patrol on that toboggan, there I was, sitting upright in the driver's seat of a motor home as big as a semi that would be the foundation for the life I had decided to live on my terms. To create a life that truly blows my hair back. We were on our way to Kentucky to begin living the grand experiment I dubbed the Radical Living Challenge.

And while we had not yet named the RV, as I took in all 40 feet and 9 inches of her, there was no doubt she was she. The floors were made of tile but looked like gray hardwood. The off-white cabinetry was made of maple. The kitchen had large, bright-white counter-tops and a modern subway-tile backsplash. There was even a tiny dishwasher and a convection oven that doubled as a microwave in the kitchen. There was a half bath that we decided would be the one my husband, Jeremy, would use, a king-sized bed, another bathroom, and even a washer and dryer. When the sides popped out, the inside of the rig looked like a 400-square-foot New York apartment. There was a kitchen table, a couch, and space for two recliners, one of which I had removed and replaced with my exercise bike. Her exterior had been custom-painted white, with splashes of blue mirroring the hues of the ocean in both bright sun and light cloud cover. We even had room enough for our two cats, Simon and Fergus (a.k.a. The Katz Brothers), to come along for the adventure. And, we had purchased a matching blue Jeep Sahara to tow behind for exploring towns and places where the RV couldn't go. Our customized license plate said it all: "RadLyfe."

RADICAL LIVING CHALLENGE:

Let's explore the differences between an intention and commitment and set the foundation upon which you will begin to live life on your terms.

Intention: An intention is the message you give yourself about what you are planning to do. An intention reflects how much and what type of energy you are putting toward reaching a particular goal or task. In this case, you will set an intention to reflect the energy and commitment you want to put toward creating your Radical Living Challenge.

Begin by answering this question: What is one thing I want to feel as a result of reading and completing the exercises in this book? This will be your intention.

Commitment: Commitment is neither looking back nor having your energy split by doubt or worry. When you truly commit to something, you don't give yourself an option to turn around and run or play the "what-if" game, meaning, "What if . . . this (or that) doesn't work out? Perhaps I'll hold back a little to be sure." Commitment based on a "what if" is not a full commitment.

What is your commitment to the process of creating a meaningful life on your terms? What does that mean to you, and how does it relate to you today? How can it support you as you walk through this process?

> "The problem you think you have
> isn't really your problem."

CHAPTER 2

It Takes More Than Fresh Air and Sunshine to Cure What Ails You

Waverly Hills Sanatorium, Louisville, Kentucky

Imagine it is 1926. Flappers. Prohibition. The golden age of jazz. Except *you* have just been diagnosed with tuberculosis.

And there is no cure to this tragic disease, and there won't be for nearly 30 years.

So, if you lived in a certain part of the country and were able to afford it, there was a five-star hospital you might go to located in Louisville, Kentucky. It was called the Waverly Hills Sanatorium.

When my husband mapped our route for the yearlong adventure in the RV we had decided to name Andi, I had assumed our first stop, the sanatorium in Louisville, Kentucky, about 300 miles away from where we picked up the RV in Indiana, was a mental hospital. However, that was a "truth" that wasn't at all true. In fact, the hospital was not only a place for TB patients to quarantine but also, according to the logic at the time, that with 20 minutes of fresh air a day, sunlight, and bedrest, you would more likely recover. In fact, the entire hospital was constructed to facilitate the flow of air, and patient rooms were outfitted with terraces onto which the staff could easily roll the bedridden to absorb as much fresh air and sunlight as possible. Even in the midst of winter. There are even pictures of the sanatorium that show patients covered in snow as part of their recovery.

And so, by 1926, the sanatorium was a sprawling five-story facility treating more than 500 patients at a time. Since closing in 1961 after a brief stint as a nursing home, the now-dilapidated Waverly Hills Sanatorium had become most famous for being home to a plethora of paranormal activity. Essentially, ghosts from the past lived there, *still*.

My version of the sanatorium wasn't a five-star hospital though. My version had wheels.

And I truly believed that the freedom of spending most of our days and nights living in Andi, just steps away from fresh air and sunshine, might resolve the challenges Jeremy and I were having in our relationship. We had been together for 13 years and married for 8. And while we had built a strong foundation, ultimately the relationship had begun to crack under the pressure of unresolved issues, particularly my role as the primary breadwinner. It was as if the more we explored what it might look like to change our life as my youngest daughter's graduation from high school drew nearer, the more I found myself insisting *he* change.

When we first met, he was a production supervisor in the entertainment industry. However, as we blended our lives and he embraced the role of stepdad wholeheartedly, he took those industry jobs less often, dedicating more time to driving the three girls to school and making lunches. Later, when the kids became more independent, he took on a part-time role as a personal assistant. But when he lost the assistant job during Covid, and his purpose as my caregiver once I began to heal from the accident, the arguments between us returned. He was unhappy. I was unrelenting in trying to fix the virus that had infected the relationship.

In response to it all, we decided to do an experiment renting an RV for six weeks. Get some fresh air and sunshine. Admittedly, I approached it as a tactic to pacify his restlessness; besides, I thought it might be fun. He saw it as a great adventure and escape. And as we journeyed through the Pacific Northwest together in the 36-foot rented motorhome, something extraordinary happened. I began to see the life I had in LA in a different light. And I found myself falling head over heels with what felt like the simplicity of life on the road; the sweet, sweet daily proximity to nature; and above all a profound sense of connection that had somehow enveloped us in taking it all on together.

But here we were, just hours into the new life we had decided to build, and I was on edge. As the wide expanse of Kentucky unfurled before us, the windshield wipers like colossal brooms attempting to wipe away the pelting rain, we started arguing.

"You are going too fast!" I said as Jeremy's tongue slid slightly out of his mouth, his eyes narrowing in on the road ahead as he leaned forward in the captain's chair, changing lanes, putting all 64 feet of us—Andi and the Jeep we were towing behind—into the next lane over.

"Stop talking *at* me," he spat back, his eyes quickly shifting to where I sat on the passenger seat, struggling to keep the laptop balanced on my knees while I kept failing at trying to connect to the Internet. He shifted his torso and shoulders even more toward the steering wheel, as if getting his physical body closer to the dash might provide him with more clarity and confidence about how to drive the behemoth vehicle that was now our home.

"This is supposed to be fun," I said, tears springing forward, the accumulation of exhaustion, nerves, and hunger. "We should not be fighting." I exhaled, sulking, keeping my eyes on the road, as if my concern might somehow protect us from the danger of driving such a massive vehicle down the freeway.

While Jeremy had joyfully set his sights on planning the itinerary and research to determine what equipment we might need, I wondered if I had agreed to the challenge for me or for him. I considered all the items Jeremy had wanted to bring with us that had been left behind at the RV dealership where we had packed all our belongings from a moving container into the RV. We had run out of room. I had been so angry, scolding him in the frigid Indiana March twilight after a day of work, looking at the mess that was all the boxes he had packed that had been piled high with the sporting equipment he never used over the years, his "Museum of Forgotten Toys." Getting rid of it all the next morning before leaving for Kentucky had been a stressful task that had also left me depleted. We had been running back and forth from the hotel we were staying in until we could leave. I had been trying to work from the cubicle

I had found inside the dealership while Jeremy had been quickly trying to stuff our things into small spaces.

But now we were here. We were on the road. I just wanted it to end, this bad blood between us. My resentments. But it was hard to just sit and be and hope we might return to a state of balance. That the year would not break us. To stay focused on the moment. To heap the past upon this so soon would be tragic. I wanted just to remember that shortly we would unhook the RV from the Jeep, grab the tickets, and head hand in hand into the sanatorium to look for ghosts.

After all, for Jeremy, this year on the road was his escape out of LA to hit his list of destinations. And we had reached the first one. And that was good.

But for me, I knew it was time to start facing the ghosts. It was time.

Two hours later, we were inside the once-abandoned buildings. Having suffered from water damage, rot, and general neglect, the plaster everywhere appeared to be crumbling. What I could see of the ceilings in the dark sagged, and most of the walls were damaged. Many windows were broken or even missing entirely, which had accelerated the decay of the interior spaces, and doors were often damaged or missing. The graffiti the vandals and thrill seekers left further marred the hospital's massive, dilapidated interior. The decay, combined with the fact that thousands and thousands of men, women, and children had died here, and rumors of ghosts, contributed to the eerie and unsettling atmosphere of the place.

As the tour guide began to share details of the morgue where we stood in the inky night, I felt something press against me. The shadows flickered and eerily danced on the walls, creating a constantly shifting landscape of shapes and forms. I shifted my weight, and in an instant turned my head left and then right and back again before I saw Jeremy standing a foot away, taking a video. Startled, I looked around to find I had been standing alone, slightly apart from the other tourists in our small group. This is when a woman appeared from a place in the room where the darkness seemed denser and who had heard my gasp. I could see her smile. "My great-grandfather died here from tuberculosis. I felt his presence walking down a hall earlier in the tour. I guess he's back," she added, laughing as her voice echoed down the cold and drafty hallway.

I certainly could not see a ghost that day in Waverly. But I felt *something*. In the final part of the tour at Waverly, the guide took us to room 502, a small, stark, and decaying patient room that was much like the other rooms we had seen. Inside there were a few pieces of antique medical equipment and a rusted bed frame. As we gathered around the guide, he told us a story about a nurse who allegedly hanged herself in room 502.

When I got back to the RV, I searched it on the Internet to find dozens of stories about what happened in room 502. Some say a nurse hanged herself inside the room because of her despair after living for years inside Waverly. Others believe it was because she had an affair with a doctor. Still others say she jumped off the roof to her death. None of them are the absolute truth. And whether we see them or not, the ghosts are there.

How to Unstick Yourself

If you do not seek wisdom and begin to question the rules of this world and rewire the neural paths in your brain that create your beliefs, you will be stuck living the same version of your life day in and day out, abandoning yourself, and your dreams. You'll be haunted by the stories of the past as an excuse to stay stuck endlessly scrolling, drinking too much wine, or working too hard caring for others or in a job or career that will never love you back, reinventing ways to write the story of your demise with the same ending every time. Stuck with those feelings of emptiness, burnout, unlived dreams, and regrets. Just like I had been.

The question is, are you going to learn how to use the "Ghosts" in your room 502 as the reason why now is the most important time to take steps to live an inspiring and meaningful life? To course correct and reclaim yourself so that you can create your next chapter?

Whatever your metaphorical Ghosts may be, and you will have the opportunity to search for them at the end of this chapter, I want you to know that they are not real. They are simply what seem like the logical conclusions to the experiences you have had in your life this far. And as such, it is important you do not let these Ghosts talk you out of moving forward in the pursuit of a meaningful life. Because ultimately, they will haunt you wherever you go until life happens and forces you to either confront them or suffer from what will feel like a life unlived.

The Ghosts of the past show up in what I call the LAICs. LAIC is an acronym to help you remember the different types of self-beliefs you might have that have formed the Ghosts you are carrying around in your head and heart. LAIC stands for:

> **Limiting beliefs:** A limiting belief is something you believe to be true that is not the truth. It's simply your truth. For example, "I'm too old to live life on my terms."

> **Assumptions:** An assumption we make is based on the idea that if it happened before, it must happen again. For example, you asked your boss for more flex time three years ago, and you think that it was the reason you didn't get a promotion. So, you may not ask for what you want now because of the belief that it will hurt your career if you set boundaries.

> **Interpretations:** An interpretation is the lens through which you experience everything. For example, if you have a paradigm that you have to fight to get what you want, you may feel that everyone, from the Uber driver to your partner's mother, is against you.

> **Committee of demons:** The Committee is simply a catch-all for the negative voices in your head. For some of you, thinking about these voices like they are simply the internalized negative voice of a parent or caregiver or any other person of influence who told you what you could or could not do. That you were not good or smart enough. Or that you were not important through their words or actions. Often we take that voice we hear and internalize it, which turns into that negative inner monologue that is not the truth at all.

Think of the LAICs as the ghost stories you want to leave behind. Reflect on the meanings and stories you have made up as a result and how they have impacted your life story.

RADICAL LIVING CHALLENGE

Consider all the Ghosts of your past. These might be limiting beliefs, assumptions, and the stories the Ghost tells you about what you can and cannot do. You may want to start by making a simple list of your Ghosts, and then look at how they have impacted you in your life overall and reflect on how they are holding you back right now from living life on your terms.

You may have a list of Ghosts, as some of my clients do when they take on this exercise, and some of you will merely have one big Ghost that seems to impact all your life. Whatever you discover, remember to look first at the areas of your life in which you feel the Ghost's voice is most active and begin your investigation from there. And finally, remember to be gentle, compassionate, and brave. We have all begun this way, and it is the first step to feeling freedom, joy, and peace.

In your journal, answer the following questions:

- What are the Ghosts in your own room 502?

- How have they impacted how you define yourself?

- How do they impact what you do, and how you do it?

"Don't let fear get in the way of your biggest dream, even if your biggest dream is your biggest fear."

CHAPTER 3

It's in the Quality of the Questions You Ask

Mammoth Cave National Park, Kentucky

After spending two days in Louisville, we still had not hit a grocery store, and as we began to head toward Tennessee, I spent the first three hours of the drive mostly in silence, distracting myself with work. Jeremy was intent on the road and navigation.

I remembered back to the day in May eight years earlier when Jeremy and I had legally married, a necessary step before the wedding that would take place in France just one month later. Hours before meeting the officiant to say our "I do's," I sang "You've Got a Friend" in a recital at the public library. As I stepped onto the stage, the weight of my vocal insecurities lingered. I wasn't a singer, but I had poured my heart into months of voice lessons. Sitting in a wood-backed folding chair as I sang, Jeremy had been my greatest champion, applauding from the audience as I tripped over the lyrics, red-faced, staring at the faces of parents there to watch their children perform. My daughter Willow, who was 10 years old at the time, had been nervous about playing her piano piece at the recital, and so I had agreed to perform too. But there we were at the library, and she was on a class trip with her friends. Jeremy had been so proud of my determination to sing regardless of the fact that Willow wouldn't perform, and the memory of his warm hand in mind as he whisked me off stage into the car to get married made me remember why I loved him so much.

While we had been in the planning phases of the "Challenge," he truly had been my best friend and partner too. We spent hours talking about where we might visit and imagining the hiking we would do together. It had been easy to put aside my fears of what living in 400 square feet with my husband might do to our relationship. For years, I had been referring to the tension we had in our marriage as what a therapist friend of mine described as "normal marital hatred."

But, I wondered, was it really *normal?* The bickering and resentment that seemed to be part of a dance we did again and again, in which I performed mental handstands and backflips trying to get him to say or do something differently? But then, after a while, I had just become good at armoring up, and as such I put each and every argument into a perfect little compartment just outside my battered heart, justifying and rationalizing my way into believing that since the relationship I had with Jeremy was better than my previous marriage, this was in fact normal and simply part and parcel of being married.

I so deeply wanted the new life we had created to give Jeremy a sense of purpose, to make him happy, finally. To make us happy together. I reached for his hand across the vast space between the two seats where we sat, and as if it were intuitive, he reached for mine, his eyes never leaving the road. I held on tightly. This was the unspoken love that existed between us. But maybe the space and routine of our previous life had kept the cracks in the marriage somewhat invisible, or at the very least tolerable. He let go of my hand and grabbed the wheel. Fear haunted me as we drove. Like the ghosts inside Waverly, always there, even if unseen.

Then, like a dam giving way to a rush of unexpected torrents, he passionately insisted we stop at Mammoth Cave, home to the worlds' longest known cave system. As the pinging in my empty stomach ricocheted off my frazzled nerves, the bickering—should we or should we not stop—began to escalate.

"It was part of the original itinerary," he said. Then, a low whisper, "It's sort of even on the way." He was committed to ticking off all the boxes on his "things to see" in America list. And since our departure had been rushed to begin with, the unfilled RV refrigerator left me more and more hangry with each passing mile. Even something like pulling over to eat fast food was no longer simple in this hulking thing, and so we drove on, arguing about whether to see Mammoth Cave.

As the signs for Mammoth Cave began to whiz past the windshield in a flurry of mottled brown and white, I picked up my phone, typing in "Mammoth Cave." Within minutes, Google and the connection I had felt with Jeremy moments before had me intrigued enough to forget about my hunger and urge Jeremy to pull off the freeway so we could explore.

Before long, we were holding hands again, this time walking the path to the main cave. The caves evolved because of rain and river water that 10 million years ago slowly began dissolving and shaping the soft limestone into the cave systems of today. I couldn't help but wonder about the very first Native Americans who discovered the system 5,000 years ago. How then, thousands more years later, scientists perfected a process that could transform the limestone erosion into providing 40 percent of the United States with drinking water. That in the absence of resistance, the flow of water had created something beautiful as well as useful. What might evolve if, like the water, I stopped resisting the conflict within and outside of me, instead leaning in to seeking wisdom from my experiences? I had done it before, and I was determined as part of the Challenge to keep living my life in alignment with this important spiritual question.

Holding Jeremy's hand, taking in the expanse of the cave, all the hunger and frustration and anger vanished, as I was beholding a miracle. Such beauty. I imagined the water pushing its way through the limestone to create the massive tunnel in which we were standing, reminding me that it was when I stopped resisting and started allowing that I experienced the beauty and joy that were the result of what had needed to be transformed.

Abandon the Script

Whether it is with our partner or spouse, boss or children, parent or friend, the thing we want to do most is avoid the pain of the feelings we are having. The fear. The worry and concern about what might happen if we change. Often, instead, in order to survive, we cast blame on others or ourselves or the conditions. Sometimes too we avoid the conflict completely by using what have been called *weapons of mass distraction*. Things that enable us to bury the pain, such as scrolling on social media or watching something on TV or online. The good news is that it is in the next piece of the first spiritual question where we can get into action. We can start to be brave, break patterns, and consider how we choose to react to the difficult and painful parts and truths of our life we want to avoid.

It says:

> *Do we ask questions about the experiences we are having in a way which unlocks our capacity for wisdom?*

Once we begin to ask questions of ourselves from a place of compassion, we can gain deeper understanding of ourselves, others, and our situations. And this is the kind of understanding that leads us to wisdom.

Understanding Wisdom-Seeking Questions

Your intellectual mind is very smart—it's the reason you are here and picked up this book! After all, you have been trained to seek knowledge and information by asking questions. All good. However, when we are doing the work of Radical Living and creating a meaningful life, these types of intellectual-based factual questions will not lead us to the wisdom we have inside us. Nor will they help us to create true understanding. And they will most definitely not create transformation. In fact, it may do more harm than good to ask these types of questions, as your intellectual mind is typically working overtime to avoid and rationalize based on the current belief system you have that you began to recognize in Chapter 1.

To even contemplate change and what it means to live a meaningful life, and to raise your awareness of what is really at the heart of what is broken in your own life, to live in alignment, we must transition into seeking a different type of question—the types of questions I had to ask to get out of the anger, blame, and too-tired-to-deal-with-it cycle that ultimately landed me flat on my back on a mountain in Canada. Questions that bring possibility and forward motion. And the cool thing is when you ask Wisdom-Seeking Questions, you will feel better because they are designed to create curiosity rather than pat answers and are asked without blame or regret! Moreover, a Wisdom-Seeking Question is one that only you have the answer to, which is also very empowering.

Here's a quick example of knowledge-based questions from the experience I described in the previous chapter with Jeremy. At first, I asked myself, "Is marital hatred normal?" Then, "Will this Challenge make Jeremy happy, finally?" And finally, "Is the Challenge going to create connection or will it tear us apart?" Those are terrifying and dramatic questions. And most important, they were questions I couldn't realistically answer.

Instead, I came up with a powerful Wisdom-Seeking Question that could shift the focus back toward listening to the inner wisdom inside me. I began to journal, asking myself, "What can these moments I keep creating with Jeremy teach me about what I need to heal inside myself?"

Understanding the Difference between External Questions and Internal Wisdom-Seeking Questions

External Questions

External questions are intellect-based and often create a judgment. They amplify painful feelings.

Why does that person _____?

Why does this happen?

Why does he/she _____?

Why can't he/she/they _____?

Why does that keep happening?

Questions like these enforce a lack of empowerment, bring the past into the present, and close down opportunities for change and transformation. Most importantly, because they are external, we can never truly know the answer to these questions.

Internal Wisdom-Seeking Questions

Internal questions are empowering and create possibility. At first, you might look at these kinds of questions and think to yourself, "I have no flippin' idea." You are asking yourself what you can learn from an experience using different words, phrases, and approaches. These types of questions invite you to reflect inwardly, and best of all, the answers are within your grasp. By asking these types of Wisdom-Seeking Questions, you can begin to see the impact of even your smallest actions and to understand the cumulative impact of them and make new and better choices throughout life. Ultimately, you are asking yourself, What can I learn from this? from a place of curiosity and optimism. Incidentally, you can also ask Wisdom-Seeking Questions from experiences in which you were successful. You will learn not only from mistakes or hurts or wounding but also from the things that have worked in your life.

Here are some hypothetical examples of Wisdom-Seeking Questions, and there are more than 100 of these types of questions available for you in the back of this book:

What *can* I do?

What's in my control here?

What can I do to get a better result?

What's the story I'm making up about this that is causing me to feel bad about myself or get upset?

What meaning am I making of the situation? What is behind my desire to _____? How might I change how I'm approaching this? What can I learn from this?

What is this here to teach me or show me?

What is one external question you have been asking?

What is a Wisdom-Seeking Question you could replace it with?

Laying Down the Love Shield

Now that you have created a list of limiting beliefs, assumptions, and interpretations and you understand the power of Wisdom-Seeking Questions, I challenge you to lean in to what it is that you have been avoiding or fear. What have you been tolerating, coping with, or putting up with? What is good enough but not great, or even ideal? Where are the places in your life where you are living life according to societal norms, pressures, or "rules"? Again, I know it may be hard to stir the pot, but remember that you didn't come this far to only get this far. Stay the course; you are on the way to a life beyond what you can imagine when you dare to approach your life from a place of curiosity and compassion.

Our avoidance behaviors are usually learned in childhood and become part of what we call your Love Shield. The Love Shield is a protective guard that keeps you in the illusion of safety. It is called a Love Shield because your avoidance behaviors are protecting you from experiencing the pain of the love you didn't receive at times in your life. You may have adopted the avoidant behaviors that develop into your Love Shield from a parent or other guardian figure. Essentially, at the time of the behavioral adoption, you had not developed or individualized enough to handle the situation at hand and/or you did not receive kind, loving support. As a result, the painful feelings were too much for you at the time. So instead of feeling the pain, you learned to avoid it and thus your Love Shield was created.

I know this can feel intense.

Like the force of water that created the awe-inspiring Mammoth Caves.

However, it's in these moments that you can breathe and allow the awareness of your Love Shield and the avoidant behaviors to flow inside and through you, knowing the power generated from your ability to be courageous and look at what is not working in your life is creating something beautiful, even as much as it might feel like it is destructive.

Here's how I like to think about it:

When you are born, the soul stitches itself into your body. It becomes part of what you are. This stitching fuses soul and body together, and then the experiences you have stitch you into life. And when you are stitched into life, you naturally become stitched into relationships, identity, your self-image, and ego. In short, the soul, which we call Essence, comes through our human form and relates to our life as it is now, moment to moment. And the more that you get into life, the more you stitch yourself to certain thoughts, beliefs, and patterns that we have been discussing. When you think about what feels right or aligned with soul, or Essence, we call it *resonance*. These are the stitches that are completely in alignment with the Essence of who we really are, and when that happens, we feel deep resonance. It's like we're connecting to what we seem to be here for. It's those moments in which the stitching is in complete alignment from soul to human form that feels fluid, natural, and aligned. For me, I describe this as living life in a way that "blows my hair back." The feeling of it all working together.

However, those are not the stitches that cause challenges, pain, or avoidance behaviors.

It's the pushing and striving. The "shoulds." The avoidance behaviors. The relationships and jobs and careers and friendships that feel so out of whack. All those stitches ultimately turn into knots that get us entangled and stuck in our lives. It can be fear. It can be loss. It can be any of those types of experiences where we haven't faced what the challenge happens to be. When that happens, a wounding of sorts happens through and in us. And, to cover that wound, you avoid and rationalize and settle, all of which create more knots and entanglements. Even fear, lack, or scarcity create knots. The need to avoid or control. The LAICS too. These are all different knots that are literally constraining our energy from flowing the way that it's meant to flow. And so, the more you untangle these knots using Wisdom-Seeking Questions, these stitches that don't work for us, the more you are literally freeing your energy and soul to channel that free energy toward creating a life that is resonant, meaningful, and fulfilling. A life that feels like you are truly expressing your Essence. When you try to make yourself happy or more content by trying to fit into what society says should make you fulfilled, however, you end up pulling those knots tighter and tighter as you search for ways to feel better. And you will continue to feel dissonance until you have the courage to ask Wisdom-Seeking Questions and listen to the answers deep within.

So listen. Really listen.

Start asking new questions.

We Begin

Step 1: Recognizing Avoidance Behaviors

Avoidance behaviors come in all sorts of packages. And the smarter you are, the more under the radar your avoidance patterns will be. In fact, your Love Shield may come factory installed with camouflage. The key is that recognizing them will be the beginning of your transformational process because it will teach what it is that you need to do to live a life of fulfillment and meaning.

As you do this exercise, understand that just recognizing that this is what you do might feel overwhelming. And when you consider all the Ghosts and LAICs you have uncovered, it can feel like all you want to do is just shut this book and give up. Opening the can of worms can be frightening. And I get that completely.

So, here's a little piece of advice. Remember that you do not have to necessarily do anything with the information you uncover at this stage of the process. Trust that the process itself will help you unwind and untangle the knots. So instead, be curious and compassionate about what you uncover. Moreover, lighten up! Because recognizing these behaviors does not make you a bad person. We *all* take on these behaviors in some ways in our life. Most important, recognize the courage you must have to surface the real problems now. And know that what you reveal, you can heal. And so, as you begin to slowly start asking Wisdom-Seeking Questions to untangle the knots and lean on the Seven Questions, you will ultimately begin to create a shift from the inside out that will lead to possibility, excitement, and a life beyond your wildest dreams.

So, that said, take a breath and give yourself a hug and a congratulations for being brave enough to look at your life from a place of curiosity. You've got this!

Circle all the behaviors that apply to you so you can start to recognize your avoidant behaviors.

Rationalizing Behaviors

Denying, creating a silver lining, ignoring, numbing out, pretending, telling white lies, coping, not speaking up, tolerating, other: _____

Addictive Behaviors

Drinking, self-medicating, cleaning, eating, shopping, smoking, sex, cheating, stealing, working, other excess: _____

Immature Behaviors

Being passive-aggressive, keeping score, taking revenge or being vindictive, blaming, teasing, bullying, holding grudges, being pushy, criticizing, other: _____

Defensive Behaviors

Being aggressive, domineering, righteous, judging others, talking down to others, needing to be right, needing to win, defending or justifying, being apathetic, other: _____

Additional Self-Harming Behaviors

Not eating, binge eating, binge and purge eating, over-exercising, physically altering self, "burning the candles at both ends," emotionally abusing, mismanaging, medications, self-medicating, other: _____

Additional Protective Behaviors

Adrenaline-seeking; impulsive decision making; attention seeking; creating messes; closing off/shutting down; perfectionism; distracting with social media, computer, or phone; seeking approval; procrastinating; caretaking; obsessing; isolating; other: _____

All the behaviors you circled are indicators that there is something else going on. Something is up for you, which will be a place where you can begin to seek wisdom!

Step 2: Ask

When you notice an avoidant behavior, you will use Wisdom-Seeking Questions to get to the root of the behavior.

- Stop or pause the behavior if you can, right then in the moment. If that's not possible, then you will want to do your inner reflection as soon as you can after that.

- Ask and reflect inwardly.

Ask yourself a Wisdom-Seeking Question like the ones listed in the Appendix or try one of these:

- Is something bothering me? What's *really* going on?

- What am I seeking relief from through the avoidance behavior?

- What am I feeling? Create a sense of internal safety by placing your hand on your heart and be curious about how you might feel. To identify how you feel, you can use the acronym SMOGS to identify basic feeling words if naming feelings is difficult for you.

  S   Sad
  M   Mad
  O   Ohmmmm (a peaceful feeling)
  G   Glad
  S   Scared or shame

Based on the wisdom you have heard through this process, address your feelings and your needs, and ask, What is it I really need right now?

Pain and Compassion

If you have any avoidant behaviors, the thing you are avoiding is the underlying feeling of what you call emotional *pain*. Therefore, pain for you can be any feelings that fall under the sad, mad, or scared categories.

What you want to remember is that pain is part of the human condition. It does not mean you are broken. It does not mean your life sucks. The truth is that part of the human condition is to experience painful things. Life is not what is projected on Instagram. Pain is NORMAL.

For those of you who are overachievers, let me challenge you. Don't forget that some SMOGS feelings can become a little too comfortable, therefore keeping you "stuck in the muck." For instance, constant or repetitive sadness can be an avoidance tactic!

What have you noticed are two or three of your standard go-to pain feelings? These are feelings that you seem to experience more than other feelings.

_____

_____

Next, identify and write it down if there is something that you have been avoiding that is associated with that particular feeling.

_____

_____

Now ask: Is there something that has been bothering or troubling me about that thing I've been avoiding? Write down your awareness here.

_____

_____

Use the Pain

Another remedy to avoiding pain is to intentionally bring in compassion and awareness. Coupled with compassion, it is a winning combination. As you seek wisdom, you will learn that it is sheer freedom to learn and grow because of experiencing your feelings, even those that are painful.

- Become aware of your feelings.
- Allow self-compassion for the feelings you are having.
- Connect to the bigger picture of why you decided to create your Radical Living Challenge by remembering that all pain can be used to remind you of the part of

you that you have been avoiding, which is, in fact, your authentic self.

Finally, here is a compassion statement you can use to get yourself through times of pain as you begin to seek wisdom from the experiences you have:

I am willing to endure this pain because I needed to know the truth of who I really am. When you utilize compassion, you can start to let go of the feeling-avoidance patterns that were unconsciously driving you and can begin, instead, to seek wisdom.

RADICAL LIVING CHALLENGE:

Make a commitment, now, to repeat the compassion statement above every day at least once per day for the next 20 days as you begin to ask Wisdom-Seeking Questions. Then, journal and reflect on the following Wisdom-Seeking Questions: What have I tried to stitch up or fix in a way to make things in my life feel better quickly? What am I avoiding healing? What does my soul want and need? What is this discontent and emptiness here to teach me? How can I use this to begin to discover who I am, *really*?

"Experiences shape us. Even if they hurt at first, they are valuable. You may even thank them."

CHAPTER 4

Don't Let a Good Life Become the Thief of Your Great Life

Great Smoky Mountains National Park,
The Appalachian Trail

As Jeremy and I drew closer to Great Smoky Mountains National Park, it felt like we had been on a never-ending road trip. The kind that sounded so fun when we were planning it, as if we would somehow jettison ourselves over the terrain instantaneously, listening to our most favorite playlist, Jeremy's fingers tapping on the steering wheel as I tapped my feet, both of us surveying the landscape exuberantly.

That is, until three weeks later and it wasn't like that. At all.

Instead, I had been stuck in the passenger seat seven or eight hours a day for days in a row, and I had heard the songs on the playlist what seemed like a thousand times already. I made my way to the back of the rig while going 80 to use the toilet as we bumped and bounced down the freeway, and Jeremy called out to remind me we were pulling over to get something I had only just learned about called diesel exhaust fluid (DEF). Something about needing to fill up immediately and to hold on because he was exiting and that we had to find a truck stop where they didn't store the DEF outside. As I braced myself for the change in speed, I thought about grabbing a snack and realized even eating fast food and my favorite potato chips had been fun the first few days, or the first week, but as I held on to the toilet paper holder for dear life, I realized I had just simply been eating like crap.

I felt so unsettled. Jeremy often complained I wasn't help-ful enough as he maneuvered Andi in and out of parking lots or a campsite we would stay in for a night with just barely enough space for a vehicle of our size. And each day, as the rain seemed to fall relentlessly while we drove, all I heard were the sounds of him clearing his throat. "Achem. Achem. Achem."

And so, after doing this several times, I felt like the ten-year-old version of myself, wondering, When are we going to actually be there? And what I meant by "there" was not only the next des-tination where we would tackle a part of the Appalachian Trail but also the life I had imagined on the road. The one in which we were having fun doing the actual living part, being in one place, settled.

Thirty minutes later, I looked at my phone. Just one more hour of driving. Tomorrow morning, I would wake up at the campsite and feel like I was home, even though we were somewhere new. I was ecstatic. I knew if we could just park and start getting into a groove for the next week, I would be less likely to lament over the tiny hairs from Jeremy's beard that seemed to leave a trail as he walked the few steps between the kitchen sink, the bathroom, and our bed each night. That I might stop chastising him, too, for leav-ing laptop cords and camera equipment strewn everywhere, while I sat in the RV firing off work e-mails and fielding Zoom calls on pins and needles, praying the Internet would hold up.

Nearly two hours later, we arrived at the national park, and as we put the sides out and fed the Katz Brothers, it didn't matter to them or to me that it had taken longer than expected or that the cloud cover and rain seemed relentless. We were here! Ignoring the gray skies, I put a floral plastic tablecloth I had recently purchased on the worn picnic bench. Andi was parked in a spot that backed up to a small stream, and the sound of the water meandering slowly by the site was the perfect accompaniment to the fading whoops of laughter coming from a group of children playing nearby at a Gaga Pit as I set the table for dinner, the pinging sound of their small ball reaching me as it bounced off the wooden frame while they playfully wove their way around each other, aiming the ball at their opponents' knees.

Jeremy sat down at the table and pulled out his phone to show me the plan for the next day, which was to tackle a part of the Appalachian Trail that crossed over what is called the Newfound Gap. This, the highest point in Great Smoky Mountains National Park, was also the highest point in Tennessee. And while hiking the Appalachian Trail had never been on my list of fantasy hiking adventures, I was excited to finally get out into the mountains and play.

By midmorning the next day, as the rain continued, we arrived at the trailhead. The mud-covered and bedraggled hikers who were most likely hiking the entire trail easily passed us as we set out on the hike together. I pulled my jacket tighter around my waist as I walked, and as the rain began to accelerate, so did Jeremy. Before long, he was too far ahead for me to see where he was, and I imagined drinking coffee in my former neat-as-a-pin kitchen and deeply missed what felt like the simplicity of the life I had left behind where being left behind on a trailhead didn't exist.

At least not in that way.

I thought about all the space in my former home as I avoided the puddles that were starting to form, thinking back to how I had defaulted into blame and rage, often being too busy or too tired to deal with the real problems. However, I thought, avoiding the puddles in life does not mean it's not raining.

I slowed my pace and focused my eyes on the path's snarly roots, taking deep gulps of air that carried the smell of dirt and mud caused by the heavy rains. I slowed even more, looking for wisdom in the trail, noticing beautiful patches of ephemeral wildflowers pushing their way through the groundcover. The ephemerals are so named because they appear above ground only in late winter and early spring, when full sunlight has the space to stream to the forest floor, just before the trees leaf out. That means the ephemerals' time to flower, fruit, and die back into the ground is short. In just a week or so, they would be gone.

Just as I noticed a fork in the trail up ahead and I wondered which way I might go, I saw Jeremy's jacket. He was standing at the top, waiting, beckoning me up toward the end of the trail. As I ascended the last few feet, I was reminded of the seasons of my life, how despite each ending I had flowered again and again. How parts of me had to die so that I could be reborn into new cycles and new seasons.

As I stood on this, the highest point of the hike, the Newfound Gap, right in the middle of both states, the light mist wetting my face, I looked out across the horizon to my right into Tennessee. I drew my hands and head up toward the small break I saw in the clouds and turned toward the left, bearing witness to North Carolina. I had been in my own *Newfound Gap* for weeks now, lamenting for the life I had left—the one of safety and familiarity—while journeying into becoming who I am meant to be now. It had been hard, messy. Downright painful. From my broken sacrum to the arguments with Jeremy over leaving Los Angeles and believing that the root of my problem was that he didn't have a job, my thinking mind was unable to recognize the limits I had placed on myself when confronting the possibility of change. I had become trapped in when . . . then . . . thinking. I had thought when I moved out of LA, in some time in the far-off future, I would be happy. Or, when my husband got a job, or when I have a certain amount of money (again, in some time in the far-off future), then I could live life the way I want to. Then, I thought, I would be happy.

However, what I think I had learned in avoiding the puddles and carefully treading over the roots while my husband walked on ahead of me, determined to simply get to the next destination on his mental list, was wherever you go, there you are. The patterns repeat. Over and over.

Unless I confronted what I had been tolerating, this way of avoiding would follow me everywhere.

I took in the beauty of both states on either side of me, understanding it all now so clearly. I smiled as Jeremy snapped a photo of me, feeling a sense of deep freedom. I had to let go of the past. That part of me had to die so that something new could emerge.

I told Jeremy the story of the ephemerals and how I needed to trust the process of my evolution as it is with nature and seasons and such. "This part of the Challenge and all its messiness along the way have been necessary," I said, my eyes brightening as I looked into his. I explained further that while it felt like I had been dormant, in all that stillness and seeking wisdom and discomfort, I had been growing.

"I have to stop comparing this life we are creating to the life I've left behind," I said. "If I don't, I will just miss the growth that is here for me." Jeremy put his arm around my shoulders and kissed my lips wet from the rain and sweat, turning me gently toward North Carolina, the direction we were heading next. There was so much beauty in the way the mist hovered over the mountaintop, and the onslaught of raindrops began to feel like healing waters. This is what I wanted my life to feel like. The Challenge was the movement and growth my soul needed and had been craving.

Do Not Let Your Good Life Be the Thief of Your Great Life

When you do this work, you will recognize the transformation is in the journey itself, not simply in arriving at the destination. I had marveled at these brilliant tiny flowers being able to grow, stretching toward the sunlight they needed to flourish in their brief life. This is the way of the wisdom seeker who lives life in alignment with the first spiritual question, seeing opportunities to grow and flower in the short time you have on earth.

Whatever it is that you are yearning for, this new thing that you want to birth, the opportunity to flower will not happen if you do not continue to seek wisdom and reach for it, *now*, in the spirit of the ephemerals.

Consider and answer the following questions as you stand in your *Newfound Gap*:

- I am creating a life I love on MY terms because I value _____

- Three things I am in love with in my current reality are _____

- Three things I am tolerating in my life are _____

You Have to Stop Playing the "Rage, Blame, Too Tired, and Too Busy" Game

Through the process of seeking wisdom, it is quite normal to feel terrified, angry, sad, or even filled with remorse that you have not tended to the garden of your life earlier. You may even have doubt that your desire to create change is the best move, especially when you believe others might think you are crazy to give up what you have. The only option, therefore, is to know that this muck is actually part of your transformation. When you seek wisdom, you are transforming the energy of pain and fear and avoidance into grist for the mill. You must stop the "rage, blame, too tired, and too busy" game you are playing between your ears. For me, I had to get that panoramic view from the top and let go of the need to be right. Of my fear. To finally pause and be present to not only what was left behind but to stand firmly in the gap to discover what it might mean to live life on my terms if I were to rearchitect it from within.

So, once you

- become aware of your limitations and knots as well as the "shoulds" that have been at the root cause of your default life,

- become courageous enough to surface the real problem,

- get comfortable with being uncomfortable and live in your Newfound Gap from a place of curiosity, and

- give up how you play the "rage, blame, too tired, and too busy" to deal with it game,

you stand in the face of your own power and the cumulative impact of your courageous decisions. This means you can begin to make better and better choices. And from this place, you can stop, pause courageously, and finally ask the ultimate question: What do I want the rest of my life to look like?

Applying the Design Principle of Empathy to Designing Life on Your Terms

For the next part of our journey, we are going to use what the Life Design Lab at Stanford University calls *design thinking* as a framework to create your Radical Living Challenge—the pathway to your most meaningful and fully expressed life. Before we define what this is for you, let's better understand the definition of design thinking. According to the experts at Stanford, design thinking is a human-centered approach to problem-solving that emphasizes learning by doing through feedback and iteration. And, based on what we discussed in the first few chapters thus far regarding seeking wisdom as much as we seek knowledge, the feedback and iteration approach lends itself especially well to the seven spiritual questions because it allows you to start where you are. We build from there.

The Definition of Fulfillment

So, let's start by understanding the definitions of fulfillment and meaning we will use in this work. Traditionally, the idea of fulfillment has become something we experience as a result of what we are doing. The thinking goes that as we are doing activities and engaging in certain tasks, we should get a feeling that is commonly described as fulfillment. And that will make us feel that our life has been purposeful. However, this model leaves the engine that drives the experience of fulfillment outside of ourselves. It says we have to *do* something external for us to find something that exists within us innately. It's why all that I had created in my life was good, but it did not enliven me or create a sense of deep fulfillment.

Here's why. Fulfillment is an energy that lives inside us. In fact, as we will discover through the exercises in this chapter, you have had that feeling in your life already. You may just not have known it or labeled it as fulfillment. And so, what we do in this part of design thinking is to get in touch with the Essence of who you are—your Essential Self—and then discover how to bring that part of you forward into the world more often than not!

Take note, there is no one thing that defines your Essential Self. Rather, it's a weaving of threads that make up your Essential Self that evolves as you evolve. And, as you continue to seek wisdom, remember the questions you ask are not meant to lead to final answers—this is not a test where you can answer correctly and get an A or win a million dollars. The questions and answers will evolve and unfold over the course of your life because you will evolve, which is why the process is iterative and why we use the Seven Questions as a consistent and constant foundation to stay or get back on course. As you go through the next set of exercises and questions, you will see that the answers can get more revealing each time you take a pass through them.

Essential Self and Fulfillment

When fulfillment comes from what is essential within us, we are tapping into our powerful core, our Essential Self. And because our Essence is not a static state, we are a being, that is *being*, rather than what we have "been." Given that constant motion, the habit of seeking wisdom and using the data we collect is paramount to living a radical life. This is the season where the buds have not yet flowered, yet the sun is there to nurture the ephemeral in you. You have a moment to flower and to fruit. Be willing to sit in the discomfort of the journey and get ready to uncover your radical life of meaning and fulfillment.

And when you can embrace the understanding that as you experience the ups and downs of life through the Wisdom-Seeking Questions, it's exciting because then *being* becomes a verb. An act of creation.

Now, let's get to work!

RADICAL LIVING CHALLENGE:

Find your Newfound Gap

In this exercise, you will review the categories on the illustrated wheel of life below, allowing a place of compassion and complete self-review. For each section of the wheel, you will circle the number that represents your current level of satisfaction. The higher the number, the more satisfaction you feel in that area.

A word of encouragement and warning before you begin:

Once, after a fight with my husband, I did the exercise you are about to do. My husband did it as well. And, in my first pass, I was afraid to rank any area of my life less than an 8 or a 9. After all, I had worked hard to achieve such "good" marks, and it was much easier to blame. I couldn't imagine more fulfillment, more fun and play, or more intimacy. You get the point. At first, giving myself permission to desire more felt uncomfortable. In each category, I had to give myself some spaciousness to dream because the desire to dig my heels in and default into the old way of thinking was strong. To that end, it may be helpful to consider not only whether you are fulfilled in a certain area of your life but rather whether you are at capacity for how much more fulfillment or joy you might be able to have. For some, they imagine what it would look like to exponentially expand that area of their life. And for those of you who struggle with giving yourself high marks because your life is far from perfect, be careful not to underestimate an area of life because ranking it highly means that there isn't room to grow.

Most importantly, give yourself permission not to know what you can't know and let go of what you think you know is possible, as the journey of discovery itself might be what your soul is craving. So, give yourself the freedom to dream. To question. It took me several versions of this exercise to engage in a truly brave assessment. So, be patient and gentle with yourself as you go.

Part 1: Review the categories on the wheel of life below. In each section of the wheel, circle the number that represents your current level of satisfaction. The higher the number, the more satisfied you are in that area. On a scale of 1 to 10 (with 1 being very unsatisfied, 5 or 6 feeling somewhat satisfied, and 10 being very satisfied), complete the following questions based on how you feel right now.

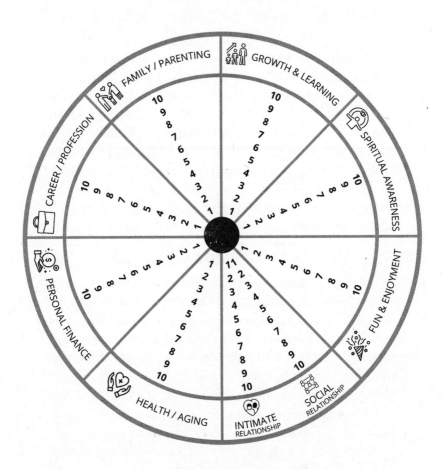

- Family/Parenting: What is working? What isn't working? For example, is your family supportive of you? Are you supportive of your family?

- Growth and Learning: What is working? What isn't working? For example, how focused are you on personal growth? Are you satisfied with your direction? Are you trying new experiences and seeking to learn?

- Spiritual Awareness: What is working? What isn't working? For example, how focused are you on spirituality? Are you satisfied with your connection to your Essential Self? What does spiritual awareness and connection mean to you? What kind of time do you make in your life to connect to Spirit?

- Fun and Enjoyment: What is working? What isn't working? For example, are you enjoying your life and making it fun? Are you satisfied with the level of activity that you do? Do you feel playful at times in your life in a way that feels satisfying?

- Intimate and Social Relationships: What is working? What isn't working? For example, are you fulfilled by your intimate relationship, if you have one? Do you feel loved? How often are you expressing love to others? Are your friends supportive of you? Are you engaging friends and socializing in a way that feels satisfying and meaningful?

- Health/Aging: What is working? What isn't working? For example, how physically healthy are you? Are you satisfied with your level of fitness? Are you satisfied with your diet? How is your self-care? How satisfied are you with your emotional well-being?

- Personal Finance: What is working? What isn't working? For example, are you earning enough income to satisfy your current needs? Are you financially set up for future growth in this area of your life?

- Career/Profession: What is working? What isn't working? For example, is your career where you want it to be by now? Are you heading in the right direction? Is your work satisfying or meaningful?

Part 2: Once you complete the exercise, journal with the following questions in mind: Why did you score yourself in each category the way you did? What's working in your life right now? Where are the biggest gaps in fulfillment in your life?

"Be compassionate for who you are and where you are."

CHAPTER 5

You've Got Mail

Bird Island, North Carolina

The sun was high in a cloudless sky as Jeremy and I made our way down a secluded two-mile-wide stretch of beach, past the last public access point at Sunset Beach, to find the Kindred Spirit Mailbox, where for more than 30 years visitors have been coming to fill empty notebooks with their wishes, thoughts, prayers, and dreams. The mailbox, its bright-red flag perched upright, was tucked into the dunes, flanked by two worn benches and tall marsh grass that moved gently in rhythm with the ocean. When I saw it, I ran ahead of Jeremy like an eager child, sticking my hand in the weathered box to find several pens and well-worn spiral-bound notebooks. I chose the notebook with mint-green pages—the color of my daughter's favorite ice cream—and a cover on which someone had drawn a heart. And then, pink pen in hand, I took a seat on the bench while Jeremy continued to stand at the edge of the water a few hundred feet away.

Soon, I was flipping pages, taking in the writing of the folks that had sat before me on this bench and mesmerized by the similarity in the dreams and desires and prayers I read on each tattered page. There were stories of grief for loved ones who had been lost and words of gratitude for legacies left. Prayers for strength and wisdom. Lessons learned. And tales of how each person had come to make the walk to the mailbox. Each one unique yet each of us kindred spirits in making the trek to this place.

I looked out into the ocean as I thought about what I might write. It was as if the mailbox itself were a box of possibilities representing the collective wisdom that was there for me if I could just see it written between the lines of each story in my life. So often, though, I had not seen the challenges and pain as part of the possibility itself, that there were lessons there for me in the journey itself that could help me grow. They were there to help me grow. Instead, I had felt trapped, like life was happening to me, something I had to fix at all costs.

I thought about how I had scurried through my day-to-day routine, frozen in fear, especially when I had been too afraid to even consider what it might look like to live a radical life. It was as if the moment I felt fear of the unknown, my rational brain took over, lamenting about what might or might not happen in the imagined far-off future. Problem-solving until my brain felt like it might break as I tried to think my way out of the problem at hand, too busy or distracted to listen to, and really hear, the wisdom inside my heart. It was as if for so much of my life, I had been trying to escape my feelings, like slamming the mailbox shut, avoiding what was inside. If I could have seen myself in that moment, I imagine my brow might have been furrowed.

But the truth was, and always had been, that amid the tide of circumstances, I had forgotten that I had the ability to open the damn mailbox.

That I had access to it all.

I wondered why these first few weeks had felt so different from the five weeks we had spent in the rented RV one year before while traveling through Washington and Oregon as part of an experiment we did to ensure living in an RV full time was the right next step. *What exactly was the problem?* I thought about the past week, how I had felt so much lighter, the wisdom I had gained on the hike on the AT creating some spaciousness inside me. At the end of the week there, Jeremy and I had effortlessly put the slide-outs in, and the cats had taken their positions on their blankets behind the recliner as we prepared to drive to South Carolina. For weeks, we had been relying on a departure checklist we had made that I pinned for easy access on my phone, but lately it felt like I didn't need the list.

I hadn't realized how disconnected I was from what I was truly capable of until I had given myself the spaciousness to become comfortable with the new routines. Things like maneuvering the 70-pound exercise bike back against the wall, clearing the counters of the few items that might slide onto the floor while we were driving, and checking that the cabinets and shower door were all shut tightly. Even helping Jeremy load the camping chairs, punching bag, and exercise bench into the Jeep. Even Fergus was getting comfortable, perching on the dashboard, looking out the expansive window as we pulled out of the campsite, Andi soon bumping her 40-foot-long and over 13-foot-tall self down a small one-lane country road, low-hanging branches scraping against her sides and roof. But even while Jeremy and I had wondered aloud if we had made a mistake in choosing this route, we couldn't stop squealing with joy as we took in the picturesque green rolling hills and surrounding winding roads and at the butterflies and birds that seemed to be showing us the way out of their beautiful state.

It was as if we had started to unfold the possibility of a new chapter, each of us moving together yet independently writing a story we had never known was possible until we hit the road. I felt a sense of what I would start to recognize as both peace and fulfillment inside me.

I focused again on being present. I watched the way my feet touched the sand. Enjoyed the feel of the sun on my face. The majesty of the birds as they circled over the sea. And the more present I became, I remembered the part of the first spiritual question that can so easily get lost in the first weeks of the Challenge to create a life of meaning and fulfillment.

I kept writing, looking at the mailbox I had left somewhat ajar. I was still stuck.

My thoughts turned toward the life we had been living since those first hours driving to Waverly and realized my work schedule had literally been turned upside down. While my business operated efficiently when I lived on the West Coast, now we were on the East Coast and would be for months. I was still working until well past nine o'clock at night to meet with West Coast clients. The travel schedule was tough too, moving every few days and staying one week in a place still felt harried, as if we had to pack everything in within an allotted time. The mechanical breakdowns strained my work flow and Internet access. The bickering over the length of time it seemed to take to do everything was relentless. Then I remembered an important truth I want you to etch into your brain.

I had not lost any freedom at all.

I had simply forgotten *we get to choose* how we happen to life, rather than remaining powerless and letting life happen to us. With this awareness in hand, I went back to the questions I had first relied on in designing a radical life lived on my terms.

On the notebook paper, I started answering questions like: *What are the core elements of my day that create that blow-my-hair-back type of feeling? How can I effectively create that on a daily, weekly, and monthly basis? What changes can I say yes to? What can I say no to for now?*

And, armed with that knowledge and my inner wisdom, I went even deeper, asking, *How do I create harmony between work and life that feels aligned with the journey my soul has taken me on in the Radical Living Challenge?*

I continued writing:

Kindred Spirit, I want to feel free. Like a bird. To do this, I will need to embrace the journey of my life as the exact one my soul has asked for. Help me to find the courage to dismantle the narratives I have in my head, all the expectations and "shoulds" I have been wearing like a lead vest. Of others. Of situations. Of myself. I thought I had left them all behind in California. But there are those that stubbornly cling to me like pieces of cellophane. Kindred Spirit, help me to remain curious from a place of self-compassion so that I can live with grace as I journey back home to myself.

I reimagined how I wanted my life on the road to be.

"I want to slow down," I said to Jeremy the next day as we cooked our dinner of grilled chicken and veggies on the propane stove set on top of the picnic table. "I want to enjoy places, linger a little."

His resistance felt palpable to me as he looked away and began staring deeply into the mushrooms and zucchini cooking in the pan, the only sound being the sizzle of the vegetables and the whoosh-whoosh of the propane as it turned into flames.

"We could do that, but we must move campsites, then, in the middle. It's hard to extend and stay in the exact same site." I was willing to compromise, and so immediately he picked up the phone with his free hand to search for a site we could move to in the motorcoach resort we were to stay at in Hilton Head if we extended three more days. And that felt like freedom.

The Cumulative Power of Small Actions

Each step along the path you are taking now here, and have walked in the past, has so much value and power, despite the outcomes. The journey itself, and even being in the uncomfortable gap, holds as much juice as the destination itself when you begin to shift your thinking into a wisdom-seeking orientation. That moment you can see that the gap you are in—the precarious time between what was and what will be—isn't a mistake or a blip or an inconvenience. It's from this awareness that you can loosen up the knots and entanglements of self-judgment and pressure you feel that your life must look or feel a certain way. Or that what you have done so far is somehow a mistake. When you are oriented that way, you cannot be free. To be free and live radically and continue leaning in to the iterative process that holds the wisdom we have gained is to know deep within that all the pain or overwhelm or confusion or even what you may have considered a mistake is part of your soul's journey. That each moment and each action of your life is part of the unfolding of your new identity, and that when you can compassionately look at life from this lens, you become a free soul winding gently its way toward a fuller expression of who you are. In living life this way, you can find peace while simultaneously being in the discomfort and pain of the Newfound Gap we discussed in the previous chapter. The magic comes from holding both experiences together at the same time.

And with this foundational mindset, you can make new choices in each situation as you design your meaningful life. Your power lies in how you show up for the challenges along the road. And in how you respond to what isn't working or what doesn't feel aligned.

This is when you remember you have choices. You can decide to start asking yourself different questions.

That's empowering. And so, remember that when you are brave enough to remain curious and listen to the wisdom inside, you have the opportunity to let it pull you toward the dreams of your deepest desires. And in this, you can be free.

For me, living on the road with a set itinerary and plans, I believed I had less freedom in my life as a result, and that somehow, I had lost the power of choice along the way. I behaved as if life on the road were a condition or a system in which I was trapped. A circumstance in which I could not make certain changes.

The power you have each day is to question every one of the rules and systems and automations you are unconsciously living by and begin to choose differently, to make adjustments in your life whenever and wherever you can along the way.

The journey of becoming what we truly are and expressing it in the life we create and the decisions we make for ourselves is the dream. It is the very experience itself that can bring meaning and fulfillment to your life. Hold on to it. Be willing to cast aside what you think is the dream and instead be present to what is unfolding and what is becoming along the pathway of your journey. Learn to be critical and self-critical in a loving way. And to know that it is the cumulative power of the actions you take moving forward that will describe the rest of your life.

RADICAL LIVING CHALLENGE:

Write your own "Dear Kindred Spirit" letter, not to be sent but to practice connecting to and listening to your wisdom. Before you write, take yourself on a walk somewhere where you can connect with an element of nature. As you walk, focus on being present as thoughts form in your mind. Notice if the thoughts are coming from your mind or someplace deeper inside you. Remind yourself to find presence again whenever you find yourself thinking or planning what you might write by redirecting your attention back to the now. Most important, write your Kindred Spirit letter from a place of self-compassion and curiosity. If you feel stuck, write as if your Kindred Spirit wants to tell you something they want you to know.

We do have power in our lives, and asking powerful questions can help us act from a place of higher consciousness more than we might have in the past.

"It takes courage to be in the time between 'no longer' and 'not yet,' as this is the period of becoming."

CHAPTER 6

Have You Ever Seen an Alligator at Walmart?

Hilton Head Island, South Carolina

I had seen signs everywhere that said to beware of alligators since arriving in the Carolinas. But I hadn't seen an alligator anywhere, despite the hundreds of miles of waterways we had walked past and driven over. But it wasn't until a few days after arriving in Hilton Head Island that I saw one for the first time.

Jeremy and I had decided to go to Walmart to pick up a few supplies, and as I jumped down out of the Jeep, the concrete starting to glint as the hot sun began to heat up the day, I saw an alligator. There it was. Hanging out between a Subaru and a Hyundai, walking over the curb and in between the tires. I tilted my head forward, opening my eyes wider, as if I might have possibly been imagining it there. And even though the alligator in the Walmart parking lot was just the size of a skateboard, it was real. Long snout, beady little eyes, reptilian skin, and tiny legs.

I slammed the door shut, putting aside what seconds before would have been a purposeful walk to the entrance. Instead, I walked toward the alligator, stopping a few feet away while Jeremy immediately pulled his phone out of his pants pocket to video not only the alligator but also the crowd that had quickly begun to gather. I stood frozen, my jaw still open, as I tried to puzzle how in the hell a gator had ended up here so far away from water. All of us onlookers were confused, standing in a Walmart parking lot, pointing at an alligator, voices rising as we wondered aloud what to do.

We had been watching the alligator for almost 20 minutes in the parking lot when I became aware of how that alligator was like the critical voice in my head, showing up when I least expected, telling me what I could or couldn't do. Freezing me in my tracks. The voice in my head that told me what I deserved or didn't deserve. The critical voice wondered what others might think of me if I dream big or live outside the box. It never mattered that I was an expert or that I had been brave before in my life; the Alligators just kept showing up, giving voice to the fear that could take me so far off course of what I set out to do.

As the ruckus over the gator continued, it was clear that its fate would not be realized for hours, and as we had other errands to do, I knew it was time to get in and out of Walmart before the afternoon was over. We wanted to go for a bike ride and go in a Jacuzzi, and I wasn't about to let a damn alligator steal the day.

As Jeremy put the phone back in his pocket, I grabbed the list I had made from my backpack, and we made our way into the store. I shook my head in disbelief at the power of that little alligator. It had stopped cars from parking. Some had decided not to get out of their cars at all, choosing to wait it out. Hordes of people had become immobilized, forgetting time or what they came to Walmart to do. Taken off the course completely. The power of the damn alligator.

I thought about how embarking on the Radical Living Challenge was like deciding to go for a swim in one of the myriad of coastal waterways native to Hilton Head Island, which is brimming with an estimated 2,000 to 4,000 alligators! I had jumped in all right, and the more difficult the Challenge became, the more Alligators there were, snapping and making me believe I wasn't capable or deserving of having a peaceful and abundant life of meaning. The voices in my head that had been the root of me comparing my life on the road to my life in LA. Comparing my husband to other husbands and other marriages, comparing myself to other business owners and other writers. And in each instance, the voice of the Alligator always had me fall short because it was there, trying to keep me small and stuck. That is until I remembered that the inner critic—the Alligator—would always be there below the surface, waiting to keep me stuck. Frozen. Not believing in what was possible.

That night before bed, the groceries and paper towels and toilet paper put away, I grabbed my journal. Yes, the Alligator had shown up several times in the weeks since the Challenge had started, but in seeking wisdom through writing, I recognized the Challenge—and thus the Alligator—was purposeful in and of itself. The voice of the Alligator had been there to bring light to the issues that needed to be resolved inside me and my marriage so that I could be free from hurts, burdens, judgments, and resentments of my past.

As I watched the lights of other RVs flickering in the night sky through the small window near where my husband and I would share the bed that night, I looked around at what was quickly feeling like home. That blend of both nerves and excitement co-existed—"nerve-cited" I had named it—and it felt like courage instead of being afraid of the Alligator. I felt proud. I had decided to jump in! I remembered walking back into my house in Los Angeles on the Sunday night after Jeremy had finished moving the remaining furniture out of the house into storage. I had just returned home from a three-day work event, and as I looked into the room that was once my office, my hands clenched the little carry-on suitcase I had brought with me tightly, I bent over at the waist, hands on knees, and began to cry. All of it gone, all of it leaving a space inside me that the Alligator began to fill, shaming me for my foolishness of letting go of the one thing that had provided security and safety: my home. In that moment, despite all the planning we had done, I had faced those beady eyes and had turned toward the confusion, pain, fear, and limiting beliefs and learned to start listening and learning from it all. And here I was!

Alligators had not changed for 80 million years, I thought. Mine were not going to simply vanish when I achieved what I thought might make me feel happy or fulfilled. For as long as I dared to live a radical life, the voice of the Alligator would challenge me. And that was living!

One Important Principle Will Forever Be Your Superpower

For most of us, change of any kind activates the Alligator. You feel out of control and can easily fall into the rabbit hole of self-doubt and regret. However, this superpower will set you apart from the other mere mortals who are relying mostly on their intellectual prowess to lead their lives, often scurrying from one idea to another, never quite knowing the next best move because of the simple fact that they are trying to avoid Alligators.

This superpower is not only being able to actively hear the voice of your Essential Self speaking to you and recognizing the Alligator is telling you a lie but also trusting yourself enough to listen to your truth. Most of you might call this superpower your intuition, and you may even have an inkling of what intuition looks like to you; however, the question I get most often is how to discern the difference between your intuition, which is the voice of your Essential Self speaking to you, and the critical voice inside your head, the Alligator.

Before we answer that question, let's talk more about those little reptilian naysayers.

To be clear, the Alligator is that little voice in your head that is there to sabotage you from living a meaningful life on your terms. Like it did for me, the critical voice will most likely show up in the moments you are in fear, especially when you are thinking about or doing something that is uncomfortable and feels pretty terrifying.

For example, when you read this book and experience a feeling of excitement, notice if at any point the Alligator shows up and tells you to stop dreaming. Or, maybe your Alligator is more subtle and just says, "Let's go eat a bag of chips right now," or, "Hey, let's just go do something else and finish this chapter later." Or maybe for you, the Alligator voice reminds you of all the e-mails you need to answer or tells you to scroll social media or watch a movie instead. Or, even more subtle, the Alligator may even convince you that you don't have any dreams or ideas about what might make your life one you don't need the weekends to recover from.

The bottom line is that the Alligator is very sneaky, and if you listen to it, it will cause you to settle, stay small, keep your guard up, and second-guess yourself, thereby directing you away from your dreams, your courage, and of course, your inner wisdom. And it will most likely be when you least expect it.

You might even be thinking you have this Radical Living thing down, or maybe it's the day that you tell your friend you are excited as a result of reading about exploring a dramatically different path in your life. And then, there it is. The alligator in a parking lot. Right when you start walking toward the border of the newest version of you, the closer you get to that border, the more likely it is that the Alligator will show up with its beady little eyes. And a crowd will gather too. All the different internal negative critical voices in your head will most likely get louder and louder, telling you what you can and can't do, what you do and don't deserve. In fact, the more changes you make or even think about making in your life, the more often you'll hear the Alligator's voice.

The good news is that all this means you are moving out of your comfort zone.

Remember, the more that you start to recognize this voice as the Alligator, the more you are experiencing an expansion in your self-awareness. And when you have awareness that *you are not your thoughts,* and that *you can separate yourself from that Alligator voice,* the more you increase your consciousness and begin to see things in a new way, free from being the victim of a life ruled by the Alligator.

Your job moving forward is to recognize that when this happens, the Alligator is lying to you, because what I had to remember was that its primary job is to keep me and you safe, and also stuck. Here are a few things that you might hear your Alligator say:

- It's not that bad. I should be grateful for what I have.

- I'm not capable of doing something like that.

- I can't do it! (The Alligator will then proceed to recite a list of all the reasons that most likely are limiting beliefs we discussed in the first chapters of this book!)

- I don't deserve it.

- I'm not smart enough to have that kind of a life.

- There must be something wrong with me. Why can't I be happy with what I have?

- Living a peaceful and fulfilling life is for other people.

- Other people will think I am crazy.

Does any of this sound familiar? Maybe you have your own set of thoughts that the Alligator whispers in your ear. Or maybe you are not sure what they are because you just haven't recognized it as the Alligator voice. Either way, like alligators in South Carolina, they are there—lurking.

Instead, you can begin to develop agency to recognize the difference between the voice of the Alligator and the voice of your Essential Self. When in doubt, pay attention to the thoughts you are thinking. The Alligator voice will sound critical and constricting, while the voice of your Essential Self will be expansive and feel like love. The Alligator voice feels dissonant in your body. You might locate that dissonance as heaviness in your chest or in your belly. When you connect to the voice of your Essence, however, it feels resonant. Aligned. Things just feel like they click. It's from this place of resonance and connection to your Essential Self that you have a direct link to your inner wisdom. And that wisdom is your superpower. When you become aware of what it is *not,* then you can begin to make new choices and move courageously forward on the journey toward living life on your terms!

Love Yourself Free

Most of the time, you believe that the critical Alligator voice helps to motivate you. Or that you deserve whatever the Alligator is dishing out. So heed my advice. Think of it like those signs I saw in the Carolinas reminding me to beware of the alligators.

If there is a part of you that still doesn't think you can change, listening to the Alligator will not help! Believing you can hate yourself into happiness, contentment, or feeling good about yourself is an ineffective strategy, as is trying to pretend that there is not a longing for something deeper inside of your heart. And while you may have used the voice of the Alligator as a strategy to motivate you in the past, think about it carefully. You would never speak to a child who is afraid or uncertain or someone you love the way you speak to yourself via the Alligator.

Instead, remember there is a new way to break free of this way of being and thinking. In fact, you can find motivation and the courage to change through your inner wisdom. Here's how:

- Recognize the voice of the Alligator as a learned way of thinking, rather than the truth. The sooner that you can accept yourself as enough, unconditionally as you live through life's challenges, the easier it will be to quiet the Alligator.

- Acknowledge the pain and discomfort that is happening while you are going through a challenging moment. Stop fighting the Alligator. Instead, be open to noticing how you truly feel. Honoring your feelings, even when you are scared or overwhelmed and practicing self-kindness and self-compassion, can help you begin to bring your Essential Self back online. The moment you begin to expand your awareness and consciousness, the part of your brain in which your adult badass self takes over can begin to operate. And from this place, you can have your own back and nurture yourself with patience and self-acceptance. When you focus on your feelings and douse your self-talk with positive thoughts of how incredibly brave you are, you can begin to clear away the energy of the Alligator.

- Stop and ask Wisdom-Seeking Questions. Finally, remember to ask and listen to the wisdom of your Essential Self to discover what the pain and discomfort in the journey is here to shed light on and what it is you truly need to be free.

The first spiritual question has taught us to seek wisdom and to develop an approach to living life in which there are no mistakes in the true sense of the word. That the journey is as important as the destination. The cumulative impact of all the choices we make has significance, and when we connect to the idea that life is happening for us rather than to us, we can begin to find a sense of safety, peace, and calm as we embark on the journey toward Radical Living.

Remember, we mean *radical* in the truest sense of the word.

rad·i·cal

/ˈradək(ə)l/

relating to or affecting the fundamental nature of something; far-reaching or thorough

You see, Radical Living does not mean you have to sell your belongings and move into an RV. Or get a divorce. Quit your job. Or move to South America. Rather, Radical Living is being brave to not only examine the dissonant energy that we feel in our life but also *invite it in*. To embrace this energy and work with it as an energetic lesson that is being generated from your soul. Radical Living is to confront the Alligators and energy that are there so the Universe doesn't need to amplify it in order to bring it forward and cause you even greater suffering.

Radical Living is a process of using the current fear or struggle or longing for something different as a way to move forward so that those darn lessons don't keep repeating again and again. To invite them in, and, as a result, in the process, you re-root yourself to a new way of being and doing your life. To live a radical life, then, is to invite change into your life and face the Alligator when it would be easier and more comfortable to follow the path of least resistance. After all, that is what most of us do.

And so, it is in the gentle re-rooting you are doing here and the deepening of connection to yourself that you are beginning to explore how you could begin to design a life that is fully attuned to your soul. To live a radical life is to be courageous and wise. And as my cousin Joan once wrote on the inside cover of a journal she gave me when I was 12, remember that when you are living a radical life, your new mantra can become "life is the journey; the destination is at hand."

RADICAL LIVING CHALLENGE:

Part 1: In your journal, recall the Alligators that have recently shown up in your life. Maybe they are limiting beliefs you may not have known were there but a circumstance or event revealed it to you. What did the Alligator say to you when this situation occurred?

Part 2: Next, imagine what your Alligator might look like. Draw a picture of it. Get some clay out if you want. Whatever you do, create that Alligator and give it a name that represents how it shows up in your life. I love the names my clients come up with for their Alligators. For example, "Mister Deflato" and "Miss Party Pooper" and "Ms. Know-it-all" to "Professor." Have fun with this because remember, the Alligator is *not* you. The Alligator voice was created to keep you safe. To keep you stuck in what is familiar, even if it is not what you want or desire. There is no need to burn or destroy the Alligator once you have identified it. Remember, these suckers have been around for millions of years. We are simply using this awareness of the Alligator voice and persona as a way to direct us to the healing work we need to do. The Alligator now becomes your ally rather than your prison guard.

Part 3: Reflect on the following questions in your journal: What does Radical Living mean to you? What does it mean to live life on your terms? What are the last beliefs you need to clear that you couldn't yet see so that you can begin to design a life you love from the place of your most authentic self?

"Are you more committed to your bullshit or your vision?"

Question 2

02 Were You, You?

In the end, the question asked of each of us is simple: "Were you true to your most authentic and essential self?" There is no question that asks if you were perfect or fixed or enough or if you made mistakes. It asks that you simply live courageously and take risks, to come up short and rise again in the ongoing quest of humanity to repair what is broken and heal the self so that you can ignite the spark of life, of what is divine inside of a life of meaning—the one that is the fullest expression of you.

Introduction to Question 2

This question asks you to repair what is broken, which requires you to know yourself. To rise up and ignite that spark of life, *despite your past.* In fact, health researcher Joan Borysenko, Ph.D., says 50 percent of your genetic makeup can actually be programmed to become resilient. And as such, this time of journeying inward to discover the truth of who you are—what Borysenko describes as the liminal place, the time between "no longer" and "not yet"—is not only a normal feeling but also sacred space. The good news is this liminal space is your period of becoming, and in it you will transform.

Radical Living Doesn't Care about Your Next Uplevel

You might be wondering what the heck this means since every person on the planet who cares about achieving talks about their next uplevel. The bigger, better version of themselves. However, what you are more interested in here as part of question 2 is traveling inward to the root of who you are to connect more deeply to your soul.

That is radical.

In-leveling means we consistently iterate while becoming more of who and what we are. Then we can design and live a life where soul is expressed more and more in daily life, all of which ultimately · creates the sense of resonance inside you. The sense that you have lived a fulfilling and meaningful life that blows your hair back.

And you have learned that the more resonance you experience, the more you also feel peace, joy, success, meaning, and fulfillment. So, as you begin to practice this new way of thinking and in-leveling through the process, you become aware of the Alligator and the LAICS, practice self-compassion, assess, and adjust from a place of curiosity instead of judgment. All with the mindset of acceptance rather than resistance.

The bottom line is this—and write this one down so you can post it somewhere you can see daily:

To in-level is to live life rather than let life live you. And as a result of in-leveling, you build resiliency.

To Become, You Must Let What Needs to Come, Come. And Let What Needs to Go, Go.

There is a Rumi quote about every human being a sort of "guesthouse." It reminds me that feelings can be "unexpected visitors" that we must welcome. The quote ends with "Be grateful for whoever comes, because each has been sent as a guide from beyond."

I love it because I imagine true acceptance and surrender as standing with my face toward the sun in a field of flowers, my arms wide open. It's an image I have used often as the graphic on a slide during weekend trainings I hold for women. I invite students at the beginning of the weekend to stand and take on this posture, to embody it fully.

Try it yourself, now.

Just stand in this sunflower posture and notice what it feels like to approach your struggles and challenges from a place of being open, compassionate, curious, and courageous.

And so, as you turn toward question 2, which asks if you have truly been who you are, you must be willing to let go of what needs to go so that you can wander into the liminal space, then allow what needs to come, to come.

Does that sound familiar? Are there parts of you that also know your striving and perfectionism come from a time when you were younger and didn't believe you were enough?

Now we can figure out who you are and what blows your hair back.

CHAPTER 7

Discovering What You Are and What You Are Not

A House in DeKalb County, Georgia

We spent a week in Atlanta staying at the home of my best friend from high school, which helped me to heal and repair so that I could become even more of my most Essential Self.

We had been on the road for nearly two months when it became urgent to take Andi into a service center for repairs. While I was frustrated that we had to adjust the itinerary, a part of her was not installed properly and was rubbing against one of the tires every time we drove, and one of the appliances was on the fritz. And since the service center in Atlanta, Georgia, was able to squeeze us in, we made a plan to stay at the home of my best friend from high school while our home on wheels was in the shop.

It was late evening by the time we arrived in Atlanta, the Katz Brothers in tow, and after a home-cooked meal, Jeremy went to bed and Jeannie and I sat down at her kitchen table to catch up. I had not spent more than a weekend with her in more than a decade. As we reminisced, her mid-length silver-blonde hair reminded me of how it used to have that swimmer's sheen as it fell down her back almost 40 years before. I shared the details of my divorce and subsequent reinvention, and she shared hers. We talked about work and motherhood and how her passion for cycling and skiing and adventure continue to be a huge part of her life. I remembered how when Jeannie and I were in high school, I wanted so much to be like her. Although it had been at least 10 years since we had seen each other, in middle age, Jeannie was still smart, successful, and athletic, just like she had been in high school. Calm. Confident and a self-described tomboy too. None of that had changed. All her movements were measured and thoughtful, like always.

I reflected on how during high school I wanted to be like her so much. The Alligator in my head at that time had been present constantly, telling me I didn't measure up. The Alligator voice told me if Jeannie was my best friend, maybe I was all right too. I had spent so much of my adolescent life burying my true Essence under an unresolved childhood longing for acceptance and approval from others. Always adapting, like the Katz Brothers, fitting in wherever I was to be who I thought people wanted me to be. The engine of my self-worth always sputtering in fits and starts, fighting for external approval and the need to make others happy.

This time, though, as I sat in the kitchen with Jeannie, I no longer felt that way. There was a natural ease between us, the cellular connection we have to a time and space in our lives. To the hometown in which we both grew up. The commonalities between us made it all feel easy, like I was at home.

Later that night, I tossed and turned, trying to sleep in a new bed, and noticed a new Alligator. It was questioning the decision I had made to sell the house and get out onto the road. I sighed audibly and adjusted the pillows, aware of my acute lack of confidence in myself and my decisions. A different version of the same self-doubt I had battled in high school. Same Alligator. Different waterway.

Unable to sleep, I flicked on the light on the nightstand and listened to the pitter-patter of the rain. I put my hand on my heart, thinking of the younger parts of me that believed if I didn't do something exactly right, I would not be loved. I whispered to the younger part of myself, as if I were talking to a friend in the low light of the bedroom, trying to let the rain outside somehow manage to fall into the parts of me that still needed a little healing.

"I know. I know," I whispered aloud to this scared, younger part of myself, acknowledging her for how hard it must have been for her to feel like she had to be perfect. How it made perfect sense she had felt that way as an adolescent, always the sidekick of the popular girl, the best friend of Jeannie. The girl who always felt less-than.

Then, an epiphany: this hurt part of me was the same part that had needed to attach to the life I had in LA in the exact same way I had attached to Jeannie in high school. As if an external condition would be the thing that validated my feeling worthy and enough. Then, I put my hand on my heart and connected to the part of me I considered to be an adult, the part of me that felt so authentic sitting at the kitchen table with Jeannie. The authentic, Essential Self that felt a strong bond and kinship with my friend. The part that felt enough and worthy. And as a result, in that moment of healing, it made the changes I was going through now feel a little less terrifying.

I had done this thing! I had made a choice. I had listened to my inner wisdom and done the empowering thing! It became clear that in living a designed life, I had to give myself permission to fail and be uncomfortable and messy because I had been making bold attempts at being *more me*! It was time for me to accept that there would be this type of polarity within me—within all of us—always. It was time to embrace and accept all the parts of me at once. And there I was, in a bedroom of a dear childhood friend, being granted a gift of healing a dang Alligator.

With Jeremy downstairs, sleeping with the cats, I leaned over the edge of the bed, picking up my knitting needles from the plastic bag stuck between a book and emergency medical kit in my backpack. Each knit and each purl became a meditative homage to the authentic qualities of my Essence I had rediscovered in the journey thus far, further silencing the Alligator. With each stitch, I whispered aloud. Knit. My vitality. Purl. My playfulness. Knit. My creativity. Purl. My passion for growth and learning. And so, it continued as I honored my desire to connect with myself and others, to adventure, and to explore things new and novel. All these parts of me that I now embraced in this moment.

In the stillness I smiled, grateful to be spending this precious time with my friend. I giggled, thinking of the Katz Brothers, of their adaptability and how in some ways they had done all this so much better than both Jeremy and me. Effortlessly making any house their home. The awareness of it all granting a moment of peace. I exhaled, taking it in. Each stop on the journey truly had become a stepping stone toward the expression and deep love of my Essential Self.

Stillness Allows Us to Remember Who We Are

So then, how is it that you begin to live life from this tender space of your deepest authenticity? The answer begins with discovering what "blows your hair back." Let me explain what that means, exactly. At first glance, some clients define this to be the experiences in life that are the high of the highs. One client shared that alpine downhill skiing blows her hair back. Another said it was jumping out of an airplane. Another shared that what fires her up is speaking on stage in front of 50,000 people. And while all those might be peak experiences that feel good and that we want to take note of, that's not what we are talking about here. While those moments in your life might surely be fun, in the context of designing a life you love on your terms, the experiences that blow your hair back for this purpose are those that feel 100 percent you being *you*. Those moments where you experience a feeling of oneness with yourself and the Universe or God. You are present. You are peaceful. You feel in tune and aligned. This is what makes you feel like you are igniting the spark of life within you, a life in which your soul gets expressed in the world more often than not.

However, before you can figure out what blows your hair back and what you are, there is one thing that needs to be discussed that will enable you to come up short and rise again. And that is to give yourself a break. This question does not ask if you are perfect or fixed or if you made mistakes. Rather, it asks you to have compassion for the parts of your life when it was really hard to be and to heal and repair so that you can be who you are in your fullest expression. It asks you to look at the times that the Alligators were running the show and celebrate them as part of your journey to right now—this moment of possibility.

In all the coaching methodologies I've seen over the years, I believe part of the reason the work I do with clients works when nothing else has before is because of this important piece. Because if we can't truly honor the part of us that didn't know what we didn't know, the part that had to handle all the traumas and hurts and challenges from the point of view of an infant or child or adolescent, or even the times that as an adult you experienced a significant emotional experience, it's really, really difficult to be who you truly are now. It's like the neural wiring in your brain decides that because you screwed it up previously, there is no way in hell it's gonna let your authentic self run wild and unprotected.

To Heal and Repair Is to Accept the Journey of Your Life in All Its Glory

In the Empathy Phase of Design Thinking, the designer is seeking to more fully understand the user of the product so that he or she can create the exact right solution for the user in the product they are designing. In this adaptation of that process, your Essential Self is the user, and your ideal life is the product. To do this effectively, now that you are able to heal and repair the parts of you that were driven by Alligators in the LAIC, you will now begin the process of identifying the specific qualities of your Essential Self to fully understand who you are designing for. And as part of that, it will help you begin to understand what blows your hair back.

To do this, you will continue being a scientist, keeping track of how energetically engaged and in flow you are in each and every activity of your day for seven days. In doing this, you will start to understand when you feel most enlivened and connected to your Essential Self. You will also note when you do not feel this way. Once you have this data, you will be able to then get on the road to creating more of these flow experiences in your life regularly, rather than having to wait for a vacation, the weekend, or retirement to experience more of these feelings.

So put on your lab coat and goggles and let's get started!

What Is Energetic Flow?

When I first learned this tracking technique by Life Design Coach Jessica Fick, co-founder of the Fioneers, I interpreted her concept of tracking energy and engagement through my own lens in which energy is either resonant or dissonant. And since I wasn't yet sure of the exact qualities of my Essence, as the user of the "product" (my ideal meaningful life), the exercise allowed me to observe myself in different experiences and tasks throughout my day. As a result, I was able to observe without judgment what felt resonant or dissonant as I engaged in certain tasks. I observed myself physically, emotionally, intellectually, and spiritually to become aware of my energy during each experience.

I like the way the Institute for Professional Excellence in Coaching (IPEC) defines energy, so we will use that for our work here as we explore the definition of energy further.

Energetic flow is a resonant, constructive energy. When you are experiencing flow, it feels expansive, fueling, healing, and growth-oriented. This flow fuels your body and your perceptions, and when you are experiencing this kind of energy, it feels as if you fully understand what it means to be alive and enlivened. The more flow energy you have available, the more you are likely to capitalize on your potential and live what feels like a meaningful, extraordinary life. Being in flow feels simple. You don't have to try. Instead, it is like electricity that flows through an electric socket. Or like ink flowing out of a pen. You don't have to do anything or not do anything because it just happens. It just is. And this feels simply like you being you. When you are tapped into that kind of energy, it creates the sensation of fulfillment that you want to create more often than not in our radical life.

Dissonant energy is what IPEC describes as catabolic energy. This kind of energy feels draining. You resist it because it feels constricting. While catabolic energy can give you an adrenaline rush or even act as a source of energy in what you experience as a stressful situation, it is disruptive because the energy required to perform the task or be in the experience feels heavy and burdensome. While you may have often relied on or become used to this kind of adrenaline and cortisol in your body, either consciously or unconsciously, the long-term effects on your peace, joy, contentment, and overall health are devastating.

When you are 100 percent engaged in experiences that are anabolic, you feel resonance. When there are elements of an experience that feel dissonant, you are less engaged, and when you are experiencing lower levels of anabolic energy, your body is catabolic.

Our goal with this tracking exercise is that once you identify those tasks and experiences that feel resonant and dissonant, you can begin to consciously choose how you want to design your life to feel resonant more often than not and use the Seven Spiritual Questions to help you live life in a way in which your set point is energetically aligned, even when you are experiencing moments of crisis or struggle and even when you are in the liminal space.

The Most Frequently Asked Question

You may find as you track that your energetic flow ebbs while you are engaging in the same activity. Or that as you begin an activity, you do not feel flow, but then somehow there is a shift, and you are in a state of energetic flow. Or that one day that activity feels aligned, and on another day it doesn't. Do not be too concerned about the blips and bumps in the road as you go. This is why you are tracking for seven days. Expect the unexpected. Instead, notice it and record the information so when you begin the next phase of this science project, that data may be useful in helping you get clear on the specifics of what truly blows your hair back.

Engagement

In order to live a life of meaning and fulfillment, then, it is not simply about creating experiences in which you feel energetically in flow. It is also about engaging in that activity in a way that feels pleasing to you. The energy just feels like it is spot-on, raw, and unfiltered you. When you are engaged, you are emotionally involved in a way that feels aligned. When you have 100 percent engagement in a task, you are not only attracted to it but also take action to set your intentions in motion.

For this purpose, you are going to define engagement as the feeling that when you're doing the activity, you are 100 percent engaged in the task—not thinking of anything else. You are not only willing to do it but also feel a sense of excitement or motivation. One note: when you are emotionally connected and energetically engaged, even if the excitement feels like fear, it feels good. For example, when my youngest daughter went skydiving, she identified that her feelings sitting in the plane waiting for her turn as fear. Yet, she also experienced a feeling of excitement. So even if you are doing something that is scary or uncomfortable, like taking on a new role at work or going on a first date with someone you are interested in, when you are engaged, you are attracted to what you're doing and able to take action.

Remember another important thing here. The goal you are aiming for is not to replicate the high you might feel after a seminar or retreat or jumping out of that airplane. An ideal life is not one in which you feel the familiar rush of dopamine 24 hours a day, 7 days a week. Rather, you are aiming to be able to recognize the energy that is *within you* that feels resonant and anabolic as a result of the tracking. Once you can recognize it, the next step will be to learn how to access it, or **Re-Source to it**, when you are in a moment of struggle—because you will be. That's life. So, while you may or may not have many of those moments as you track your time in the next seven days, which I will explain below, the objective of the exercise is to begin to notice what in your life feels closest to that feeling and what feels like it is absolutely not.

Tracking Energetic Flow and Engagement

For seven days as you experience your tasks and activities, note whether or not this activity or circumstance diminishes energy or enhances your energy on a scale of 0 to 5, 5 being a state in which you experience high anabolic energy and feel 100 percent energetically engaged, and 0 feeling like a giant "ugh." To help you identify where you fall on the scale, consider the following:

- "I have to" or "I should" can feel like a 0 or a 1.
- "I need to" can feel like a 1 or 2.
- "I want to" can feel like a 2 or 4.
- "I choose to" can feel like a 3 or 4.
- A 5 feels like you are 100 percent engaged and experiencing energetic flow.

Remember that this framework is a suggestion. As you become aware of yourself in these experiences, also notice what you feel in your body. Does it feel heavy or light or somewhere in between when you engage in that task or activity? What emotions are you feeling during the experience? Does this activity feel spiritually connected to one of your core values and therefore feel like you are Goldilocks finding the bed that feels just right?

Use the chart below as a template to track everything you can, remembering that some days are typical, and some are not. Because you are doing this for seven days, the intention is that you will get a sampling of what your life feels like more often than not. Here are some other suggestions for the process based on the clients I have worked with and the questions that often come up.

- Do not overthink it or overanalyze the exercise. Your answers do not have to be perfect. Just become aware and remember that done is better than perfect. Also remember that a 5 doesn't have to be a perfect experience. I have had some clients tell me that because they are accustomed to the performance review process and that some managers or bosses believe 5 is always and forever something to work toward, they are hesitant to label any activity as such. I say phooey to that. If it feels amazing, give yourself the gift of a 5 and let self-doubt and old programming float out the window. Similarly, if you have worked really hard in your life to be even-keeled and every single thing feels like a 3, this is the time to be observant rather than judgmental. Notice what you notice and be assured that in the next chapter, you will be making some choices about what you have noticed in this process.

- Be consistent, curious, and self-compassionate as you do the exercise. Continue asking Wisdom-Seeking Questions and practice managing the Ghost and any of the LAICS that arise. If you can't string together 7 days in a row, experiment with stopping and starting over the course of 30 days, remembering this book is as much a guide and workbook as it is something to read straight through. Give yourself permission to learn from the process itself, not just the data you collect while tracking.

- You don't have to do anything with data now. Later on in the process, we will use the information to help us identify qualities and traits of your Essential Self. And if you don't feel like completing the tracking, you can continue with the process using the data you collected in the Wheel of Life Exercise. It will require you to guess, however, rather than be more exact.

- You can use the sample tracking sheet in the book as a reference point; however, you can record your data in a journal, on your phone, or on Post-it notes. Some people prefer to track as they go, and others do it at the end of the day, using their calendar or their memory to revisit what their day felt like. Figure out a system that works for you. However you choose to keep track of your data, it should only take you 3 to 5 minutes to do this at the end of your day or just 15 seconds if you rank after finishing an activity or task!

- This does not have to be hard.

- This bears repeating: you can continue reading while you do the seven-day experiment; however, you may want to revisit certain chapters once all your data is collected.

RADICAL LIVING CHALLENGE:

Step 1: Track your energetic flow and engagement for seven days.

Step 2: After seven days of tracking energetic flow and engagement for each and every action and activity, answer the following questions in your journal.

- What do you desire to do every day? Every week? Every month? Every year?

- Reflect on a recent day that felt good to you. What did it feel like? How did you feel? Bring to mind the elements of it. Consider the following: What were your emotions, what were the social conditions? Was there a connection to a core value or was it spiritually aligned? Was it intellectually stimulating or were you bored? In what environment did it take place? Consider not only the weather or physical space you were in but also temperature, time of day, lighting, noise, equipment, clothing, technology, and so on, and reflect on why you think it felt that way. Who were you with? What were you doing? When did you do it? Where did you do it? Why were you doing it? How were you doing it?

- What awareness and insights do you have so far on your energy and engagement tracking?

Step 3: Using the data points from your own Energetic Engagement and Flow Exercise, make a list of all the activities you found energizing and engaging, where you felt in flow and ranked 4 or 5.

Tracking Engagement and Flow
(do this practice daily)

	Activity	Engagement (0–5)	Flow (0–5)
❶		☐	☐
❷		☐	☐
❸		☐	☐
❹		☐	☐
❺		☐	☐
❻		☐	☐
❼		☐	☐
❽		☐	☐

"It is not about coping or finding the silver lining
in what is good enough; it's about creating
a life that blows your hair back."

As a reminder, here are the definitions of Engagement and Flow:

The definition of *engagement* is when you are 100 percent energetically engaged. You are willing, bought in, and motivated to do what you are doing or about to do. You are attracted to what you are doing, pleased by it, and emotionally involved and excited about it. You are committed and courageous, even when there is fear. Energetic engagement also includes taking action to implement.

With *flow,* you feel like you are in the zone, time stops, and you feel present. You are filled with peace and joy; you are in your zone of genius, totally in your Essential Self.

Once you complete the tracking below, you will use the data in the next chapter to begin to uncover what *truly blows your hair back.*

CHAPTER 8

Design Your Life on Earth to Be a Reflection of Your Soul

Austin, Texas

A few weeks later, in Austin, Texas, my daughter Rayna and I shared one of my favorite rituals as a full-time RVer—walking in the moonlight through the winding roads of a campsite. Although we were staying relatively close to the city, the moon was bright and high in the sky as the lights from different kinds of RVs—the fifth wheels, travel trailers, and camper vans—lit up the pathway. I was excited as I explained the differences between each of the vehicles, squeezing Rayna's hand as we walked.

"Look!" There stood a behemoth bull that had come to graze near the fence bordering the campsite. Both of our jaws dropped open. We stared at the bull, its neck and head bending down gently, lazily watching the both of us, chewing, an assurance all is good in the world. We stood together silently, looking into those big black eyes as he looked up into ours. I thought about the fence between us and the bull and how living a radical life had involved taking down so many fences in my life. Fences that felt like they kept me safe, yet really had been keeping me fenced in, feeling trapped and powerless. And how, in some ways, in order to tear down fences and live a radical life that feels boundless, I had to put a few new fences up because living a radical life is often not necessarily convenient for the people I love, and others. Building fences. Taking them down. That all required something more than willpower or bravery itself.

"Remember the night we said good-bye to the house in LA?" I said, both of us looking up into the night sky, conjuring up shared memories of the little gathering I had hosted in the fenced-in backyard that separated my house from the neighboring house just days before we moved away.

"There is something bigger than us out there, Rayna," I whispered, "God, Universe—whatever you want to call it. When you said that night the house in LA had simply become an emotional museum for you and your sisters to visit, and that I didn't need to keep the museum open for the three of you anymore, you gave Jeremy and me permission to leave that fenced-in backyard and that fenced-in life in LA. You did this without even realizing it. And now, here we are together in Texas, having had an amazing night eating Texas barbeque, singing karaoke, and now watching a freaking bull underneath a starlit night."

"Proud of you, Mom. So proud," she said, turning to give me a hug as the bull began to turn away, as if he had known his work was done in creating the moment.

I had done something bold in leaving what had been her childhood home, and now sharing the experience with her felt exactly perfect. Her words months ago had freed me from some of the guilt that night in LA, and to have her be part of the life I was living on the other side of the fence felt like a gift from the Divine.

As we watched the bull fade into the distance and talked more about the idea of fences, I began to feel the gratitude in my heart expand and then radiate out from my heart center through my whole body, down to my toes and all the way to the crown of my head, my hand entwined with my daughter's.

I let that gratitude extend to the space around us as if I were a radio antenna broadcasting gratitude and heartfulness out into that space. I allowed my awareness to follow my heart's energy and its broadcast as if I were reaching out farther and farther into the vast open space.

Then, watching the colors of night fading in the Texas sky from deep purples to deep blues to deep midnight and ultimately the blackness of deep infinite space, I felt the vastness of it, all around us, holding me and my awareness in its embrace.

That moment in the road at a campsite in Texas, staring at a bull with my daughter's hand in mine, what a glorious moment of resonance. A moment in which I felt the fullest and most authentic expression of my Essence. Me. My soul. The Universe. One.

This is what it is to experience radical faith.

It's Not Always Butterflies and Bulls

Having radical faith is your ability to grow fully present in a moment, remembering you are held by the embrace of infinite space surrounding you, even when you take away the fences that you think are keeping you safe. And even when you have to put up a fence to break free from the expectations of others so that you can live life on your terms, it's not always quite so obvious.

For example, the week in Atlanta had initially felt like the Universe had forced us to take a wrong turn. But ultimately, I remembered questions 1 and 2 throughout the week, half praying, half meditating and remembering the ongoing quest of being human is, in fact, a challenge.

And as such, I want to remind you to *expect* to experience challenges as an almost everyday occurrence.

Specifically, when:

- You get what you don't want.

- You don't get what you want.

Think about it. It happens all the time.

Traffic, for example. You don't get what you want, and you are late. You bang on the steering wheel, cursing the other drivers. The hotel you hoped to book has raised their rates. You get what you didn't want, and you complain to your friends. "I don't have time for this shit," you whisper, slamming the lid down on your laptop.

And then sometimes you get what you don't want, and you must respond to that.

The journey is to understand that as long as we are attached to expectations of how *we think* it should be, we will experience stress. And that stress manifests itself in the form of worry and anxiety, anger and frustration, sadness, or any other of the emotions that we typically do not want to feel. This is why a critical piece of question 2 requires us to become courageous and willing to hold those feelings *alongside* radical faith.

I understand radical faith to be trusting in:

- The Divine, which you can make to mean God or Universe or a Higher Power or whatever feels right to you.

- Yourself.

- The Essential Self you came into this life with, which is divine in itself. When we are in faith, there is recognition of your divine self.

The moment I had of self-compassion in which I healed the voice of the Alligator in Atlanta and the night I shared with my daughter in Texas are examples of how radical faith can help you find peace in the chaos of becoming you. If I could have more easily accessed radical faith during those moments of stress and upset along the way and trusted that it would ultimately unfold for the highest good, I could have avoided so much guilt, angst, worry, and bickering. I could have experienced peace in all the chaos.

Ultimately, question 2 reminds us that as humans, we will often fall short. It does not mean that there is no hope for us or that we must give up. Instead, the question tells you to rise again to repair what is broken and heal the self. *That is the journey of life.* When you are in radical faith, you can allow yourself to connect even more deeply to your vision of a meaningful life lived on your terms.

How Can You Create More Meaningful Moments in Your Life?

Now that you have completed or are in the process of tracking your energetic flow and engagement, you can start defining what exactly blows your hair back, remembering this is not defined as those adrenaline-type of highs you may experience when you engage in certain activities. It is, however, defined as moments when you are authentically being you. Energetically in flow and engaged!

Now, if you have only tracked for a few days or are waiting for the perfect time to begin tracking, here's an important announcement: *Life is always going to be atypical.* So here are some frequently asked questions regarding time tracking some clients have asked that may have more to do with procrastinating than being unsure.

I am injured. I'm normally more active. Can I wait until I'm back to my regular routine? This a great question. For example, if I were to track time when I was recovering from my ski accident, it would have looked different than when I tracked it a year later. That said, if your injury is chronic or has been going on for a month or two, I recommend you track your time as it is, knowing you can come back and track anytime when you are feeling better.

I am going on a vacation. Isn't the point of the exercise to track when I'm in my regularly scheduled programming? Unless you are going to vacation for two weeks, track one week on vacation and one week in your regular routine. All data is good data. And, if you are traveling for the entire two weeks, track what you can and add a week of tracking into your data upon your return.

I'm feeling kind of blah, my kids are sick, and I'm spending all my extra time taking care of my elderly parents. Can I wait until I feel better? Until I'm less busy? Until things get back to normal? The answer here is a clear no! The point of time tracking is to show you exactly how little engagement and flow you have in your life.

So, if you don't love the data you collected or you are not sure what to do because now you feel worse than before, remember question 1 and ask yourself a Wisdom-Seeking Question, such as, What is it that I need to believe in so I can design a life of more energetic flow and enjoyment? Or, What is the truth I need to remind myself of so that I can stay engaged in the process of life design? The Alligator voice will always come rushing back in to tell you what you can and can't do, so it's up to you to remember that your life is a blank canvas. And even if you believe that you can't make money from the things that blow your hair back or that it's irresponsible to even try to live a life that blows your hair back more often than not, you are letting the Alligator run the show.

So just stop it, *now*.

At the end of this chapter, you are going to learn what to do with the tracking data you have collected, so if you haven't done this exercise yet, don't worry. You can do one of two things:

- You can complete this chapter with the understanding of what you will do with the data once you have it and then go back and track and complete the homework for this chapter.

- You can use the data you collected in the Wheel of Life Exercise and use your best guess of what in that part of your life feels like flow and engagement and what feels like it is draining energy. Sometimes done is better than perfect!

How to Be True to Your Most Authentic and Essential Self IRL

Once you have started to track your energetic engagement and flow, you begin to notice what it feels like to be aligned with your Essential Self, a process I call *soul tuning*. Those moments of complete flow and engagement are you being more *you*. And then, the invitation is to consciously create greater moments of resonance with your Essence in all parts of your life on a consistent basis. This is what I call *being true to your most authentic and Essential Self*!

There are two key principles you will use as a guide to turn this spiritual concept into something you can realize in your daily life.

Embodiment: Being embodied can be understood as the physical experience of your soul, what some experts would call a *somatized life*. To embody your soul in your physical body is inherently organic because you are energy, and thus it includes thinking, relating, feeling, yearning, acting, and the social self. The questions become, What energy are you embodying when you are being? Is your embodiment resonant with your Essence?

Think of it this way: Embodiment is the being of your Essential Self within the container of your physical self. It is an expression of your soul through physicality, voice, and action. Embodiment is the synergy between the thoughts, feelings, and being you, your divine Essential Self. Together it results in the energy of having— the *having* itself. The experience itself that you are experiencing.

When you embody your Essence and are experiencing resonance, you are taking advantage of the neuroplasticity of the brain that allows you—at any age—to rewire neural pathways. This creates a new identity and understanding of yourself. It is through this expression of self—your physical, emotional, mental, and spiritual self—that you create changes in your life, internally as well as externally. The changes you make daily as you aspire to create more experiences where you are in energetic flow and energetic engagement will loosen the knots and entanglements, thus anchoring you even more deeply to your Essential Self. And as we go through these experiences, you can course correct by using the spiritual questions as your guidelines. This in itself is the in-level, the virtuous cycle that is Radical Living.

As you can see, this is very different from how you used to live life before engaging in this process. The old way of being is to stay stuck, tied to the old identity and ways of reacting to stressors. That feeling I described as being stuck in Alice's Wonderland. And that way of living is experienced as being stuck in a vicious cycle.

So, when you think about embodiment and how to create more moments of magic and flow, consider how you show up in the physical world. In resonance or dissonance? You can choose to embody the old beliefs and default patterns and limitations and the voice of the Ghost, staying stuck and avoidant in a never-ending vicious cycle, or you can aspire to rise up and repair what needs to be healed as you take on the physical form of your Essential Self. Is your focus on what you don't have, or can you effectively shift the focus on the energy of your Essence within?

The second principle is Action.

Action is defined as both *being* and *consciously doing* to create greater resonance with your Essence in all parts of your life on a consistent basis.

Without taking action, information and awareness alone are not transformative. Action is the embodiment of living courageously. When you are in action, you are willing to experience the discomfort that accompanies living an enlivened life while seeking wisdom about the experience. The action you take is what brings about your transformation and the tangible result.

Without action, there can be awareness; however, we cannot create a tangible result of our desired dreams and goals. Without action, we stay attached to the knots, entanglements, and default way of living our life. And, without action, we cannot execute our wisdom. We are not in the pursuit of being who we truly are. And inside that, we are not fulfilling on any of the concepts embedded in question 2. There is no "new level, new devil."

Action is the embodiment of BEING your Essential Self in the day-to-day of your life.

Action is the difference between the life we could have and the life we choose through action or INaction.

Action is taking the principles and skills of the seven spiritual questions and putting them into the world in a way that is resonant with the energy of our Essence.

Action creates energy and expansion.

And, moreover, action is the expression of our resilience.

Action is specific and tangible. Consider how you show up for yourself. What routine do you have? How do you practice self-care, or not? How do you show up for people in your life? Do you respond from a place of your Essential Self that is healed and whole, or do you react and act based on the Ghost? To summarize, you are choosing the life you want through the actions you take. And the ideal is to be in action of the principles and the skills of the Seven Questions, putting your Essence into the world in a way that's resonant with the energy of who you are.

So, let's discover more of what you are!

The What, the How, and Your Core Motivation— An Introduction to Soul Mapping

So, back to question 2: Were you, *you*?

By now, you may be getting an idea of what are the qualities of your Essential Self. And as you continue to tune in, the question you are exploring is not, Who are you? but rather, What are you? By asking "what," you can begin to see yourself as a being expressing resonant, anabolic energy through the fullest expression of your Essential Self, or not. You can focus on how you bring the *what you are* to *what you do* through embodiment and action. And you will do this using the data from your energetic engagement and flow exercise to create an idea of what your ideal day, week, life, and years look like. I call the What, the How, and your Core Motivation a Soul Map.

Once you are clear on the What, How you best carry out the What, and the Why behind What and How you do it that is aligned with your Essence, you will begin to use this Soul Map as a framework for a life lived on your terms that blows your hair back!

A note: I adapted this Soul Mapping process from a process I completed with Jessica Fick, the co-founder of the Fioneers, as well as through the principles of Design Thinking at Stanford University. In this process, you will examine more closely patterns of resonance and dissonance within to discover the core qualities of your Essential Self. Ultimately, your Radical Living Challenge will be to take on experiments and explore ways of bringing this blow-your-hair-back energy into your day-to-day life. Plus, doing it this way ensures you set aside your conscious and unconscious assumptions about yourself in order to gain even deeper insight into your true Essential Self and your needs.

Let's go!

Step 1: The What

The *what* is what you are doing when you are in flow and energetically engaged. This is what you are doing when you are living life on your terms.

Using the data you collected from your Tracking Exercise in Chapter 7, make a list of what activities, actions, and things you were doing that you ranked a 4 or 5—those things you found energizing and engaging. Ultimately, the outcome for this step is to have a list of activities in which you were highly engaged and experienced energetic flow. Those things you want more of in your life.

Let's see how one of my clients completed this exercise after synthesizing her time tracking as an example:

What I enjoy:

Problem-solving, giving, coaching, teaching

Live music, arts, research, travel

Making an impact, collaboration energy

Step 2: Next, Find The How

For each experience on your list, answer the following reflective question for each one:

How was I doing it? Be specific. For example, what were the conditions? Consider the following:

- What was your environment like?
- Were you intellectually stimulated, bored, overwhelmed, or something else?
- Did the experience feel aligned with your core values?
- How was the experience for you from the perspective of your physical self, your body?
- What were you feeling vis-à-vis your emotions?

- Socially, did it feel too like much or just enough? Was it a small group or a large group? Was it a one-to-one experience? For example, when I did this exercise, in some instances, I ranked cooking a 5 and in other contexts only a 2. I learned in this process that when there were other people in the kitchen and there was music playing and conversation was flowing, I was in higher levels of energetic engagement and flow. However, when I was alone and others were in a different room of the house, waiting for a meal to be served, I did not feel engaged or in flow, and therefore ranked it a 2. This part of the exercise allows you to consider how you best carry out the What.

Step 3: The Why

In addition to understanding *how* you best carry out *your what,* the *why* will help you identify the core motivations or values that are in play when you are highly engaged in your life. For each experience on your list, answer the following reflective question:

Why were you doing that task or activity? What was its purpose? For example, was it centered around connection, community, traditions, legacy, or play? Was it connected to your purpose or passion? In my example of cooking, I ranked it a 5 when I felt connection. Or when I was preparing a holiday meal because I value traditions and family time. For some, Why included words like *impact, collaboration, recognition,* and *connection.*

Be as granular as you can, and do this for each activity and experience that you ranked high in energetic flow and engagement.

Step 4: What Is Energetically Draining?

Now, make a list of the activities that you found energetically draining or that didn't hold your attention or felt forced. These are going to be activities that you ranked between 0 and 3. Then, repeat steps 1 through 3 above, answering the questions about those activities that you ranked as low engagement and energetic flow.

Step 5: Putting It All Together—
Creating Your Soul Map

Now, using the data you collected from steps 1 through 3, create a list of what you enjoy, how you best carry it out, and your core motivations. This is important, as you are now becoming closer to understanding your ideal resonant life in which you feel aligned to your Essential Self.

Did you see any patterns that you can draw from your tracking about the What, the How, and Your Core Motivations? Notice how you may have felt present in those experiences you ranked as 5s.

When the client answered this question, she realized that different circumstances elicit different parts of her Essence. She concluded the exercise with this list of qualities and characteristics:

Curious
Introverted extrovert

Takes a minute to be comfortable until I have done reconnaissance of my surroundings

Need spaciousness—physical/emotional/
mental—to process and refresh

Persistent
Intelligent
Loyal to those who support me
Quietly emotive and passionate
A curator of experiences

She also recognized that when she is the center of attention, it can be dissonant if she needs that attention as validation to disprove the Alligator's voice. And when that happens, she moves out of Essence and into anxiety and worry. She also noted that in certain cases, she is also dissonant because she stays in things too long when the core motivation is to win versus satisfaction or enjoyment. Can you see how this discernment is helping this client to better understand herself and to have awareness about how she can better design her life?

Other clients have had additional awareness in going through this process, which you may relate to. Things like recognizing activities in which they felt obligated to do something, or had to do something, there was little energetic flow and engagement. From mundane household tasks to medical appointments, the tracking created the opportunity for each one to reflect on their core motivations. Conversely, activities clients chose to do, or felt lucky to be able to do, ranked high. Some clients noticed how core motivation can change flow and engagement even though they were engaging in the same activity. And in many instances, the process surfaced new Essential Problems to tackle as they designed life on their terms.

As a result, when my clients and students do this reflection, they usually spend at least a few days reviewing it and pondering. In fact, when this client began her reflection, she didn't even have that much written in the boxes on the worksheet for What, How, and Why. However, upon journaling and reflecting, over the course of a few days, as her thoughts percolated with self-awareness, she gained more and more clarity.

So, I recommend you do this exercise over a few days at least, as it requires you to seek wisdom as you reflect on the Wisdom-Seeking Questions embedded in the exercise. Allow the thoughts and feelings the space to bubble up rather than trying to cram through it. Notice the Alligator or any limiting beliefs or "shoulds" as they pop up and continue to practice self-compassion as you are Embodied and in Action of question 2.

Finally, remember: you get to choose what you want to carry forward in your life and create more of and what you will begin to leave behind. Trust the process as it unfolds in the pages of this book. The objective is not necessarily to completely blow up the life you have now and rearrange it to align with your Essential Self. Instead, invoke radical faith and continue to be curious and courageous as you get to know what you are.

RADICAL LIVING CHALLENGE:

Step 1: Using the data collected from the Time Tracking exercise, make a list of all the activities that you found energizing and engaging and when you were in flow. These are activities that are ranked 3, 4, or 5. Pay particular attention to those that ranked 4 and 5.

List:

_____

_____

_____

_____

Step 2: Then, for each activity, answer the following:

- What was I doing?

- How was I doing it? What were the conditions?

- Why was I doing it? What was its purpose?

Step 3: Using the data collected from the Time Tracking exercise, make a list of all the activities that you found draining or that didn't hold your attention. Where did it feel forced? These are activities that are ranked between 0 and 3. Pay particular attention to those that you ranked as 3.

List:

_____

_____

_____

_____

Step 4: For each activity, answer the following:

- What was I doing?

- How was I doing it? What were the conditions? (e.g., what environment was I in? Was I outdoors? Indoors? Was I in a crowd or gathering with a small group, or perhaps one on one? Was I overwhelmed, overstimulated, or was I bored? Or, was it intellectually stimulating to me? What were the sounds? Was it a loud room or peaceful?)

- Why was I doing it? What was its purpose? Was there a deeper, core motivation behind it that felt resonant?

Step 5: What patterns can you draw from your daily tracking about your What, How, and Why? What were you doing? How were you doing it? What is the why behind it? This information will become your Soul Map!

Reflect on your answers and complete the following reflective journaling to get a clear understanding of what your Soul Map looks like:

What I enjoy:

How do I best carry out the What and the Why?

What is my Why? My core motivations are:

Based on what you observed during the moments in which you experienced high energetic engagement and flow, how could you describe the characteristics of your authentic and Essential Self? (e.g., sassy, perceptive, loving, clear, funny, fun). You may want to also include any of the insight you gained in Chapter 7 as you considered your ideal day, week, month, and year. Or the days that you tracked that felt especially awesome. Use these questions and prompts as a journaling exercise so as not to be limited by list making.

How do you feel in those moments of high energetic flow and engagement, when you are connected to Essence? (For example, joy, peace, love, empowered, silliness, creative, and intuitive.)

What keeps you from being in Essence?

_____

_____

_____

_____

_____

The qualities I have identified thus far of my Essential Self are:

_____

_____

_____

_____

_____

Question 3

03 Were You Radically Honest with Yourself?

This question is not about believing in God or Universe or faith, following the Ten Commandments or a certain set of rules, or even achieving success. Instead, it asks, "Did you deal honestly in your business?" Upon examining the text carefully, this question is not just about business. It's about honesty, integrity, and faithfulness, because if you are not really honest when it comes to the decisions you make with money, the question becomes whether you can be trusted to be honest with yourself and others.

Introduction to Question 3

Congratulations! Now you have created your Soul Map—a list of *what* you enjoy doing, *how* you prefer to do it, and the *why* behind your core motivations, which when all three combine, create experiences that blow your hair back.

This is exactly why you are ready to dive into the next question, which is a bit tricky. But, now that you understand your Essential Self in a new way and have become more adept at asking Wisdom-Seeking Questions, you can handle it.

Let me explain why this question is a bit tricky.

In its original form, according to the Talmud, this third question was asked first at the Heavenly Tribunal and specifically asks whether you have been honest in business. Perhaps this is because the sages understood that as humans, it is in our nature to prioritize our own interests foremost, especially when it comes to our finances. To make sure we have enough of the moolah for ourselves. And then if we don't, we might be tempted to take advantage of others, lie, be deceptive, or cut corners. So, in its original form, the question supposes that if we can be honest in this regard, it's more likely we can navigate the rest of our life from a place of honesty. However, upon closer inspection of the text, this question is not simply about business. Or ethics. As we have discussed, this framework is not meant to serve as an inventory of how your mortal self has performed during your lifetime. Besides, we all keep track of ourselves at some level already. That's why you are here.

Rather, the intent of these questions is to ask how you have engaged in the evolution and development of your soul, your Essential Self, and the impact you have made on the lives of others because of that journey.

And if the thought of that sends a shiver down your spine, you are not alone. Most of us have been conditioned to measure or live by metrics that largely are out of our immediate control, which is why we are always thinking we should do more, work harder, and get more stuff.

However, here, you will look beyond honesty with others in the typical Ten-Commandments-sort-of-way and instead dive into the concept of radical honesty with self. The question asks, *Do you look deeply within* to examine what it means to be in integrity with yourself?

Whether you consciously realize it or not, when you are radically honest with yourself, you are aligned with your deepest values. And when we are not honest with ourselves, we fall out of integrity. And that leads to the nagging feeling of discontent you have in your gut. Or the voice ringing in your ear that helps you rationalize, intellectualize, and cope with situations that just don't feel right.

That's why radical honesty is tricky.

We get really good at coping. And as a result, you must be willing to be courageous and dig deep into seeking wisdom to acknowledge your innermost truth by listening to your Essence in your stillness practices. The goal is to ultimately be able to discern when you are being honest with yourself and when you are being dishonest. When I work with clients, radical honesty takes finesse to gently begin to see the truth. You must be patient. Brave. And you must make the time to stop and listen to your Essence. Because, in some instances, this is the truth you have been avoiding for a very long time, if not for most of your life.

CHAPTER 9

Getting Real with Yourself and Others

Ruidoso, New Mexico

This question of radical honesty showed up for me over the next few weeks of traveling in the RV. After saying good-bye to Rayna in Austin, Jeremy and I tackled a two-day marathon to get to Ruidoso, a small town located in the Rocky Mountains of southeastern New Mexico. I felt unsettled again, and I wasn't sure if it was that I didn't want to see the truth or just didn't yet have clarity about what it was that kept me feeling off balance. I had still not managed to get into the groove of packing lunches on driving days, so on the evening of the second day, after surviving on mostly protein bars and nuts and popcorn for almost 48 hours, Jeremy finally inched Andi toward the entrance gates of the RV motorcoach resort where we were going to stay for the week.

As we slowly drove past what appeared to be well-appointed track homes lining the streets, I knew we had made a mistake. I could see the heat rising in Jeremy's neck, and rather than let him know what I was thinking, I exhaled a long and arduous sigh. I knew these gates were not the entrance to the motorcoach resort and that we had somehow become trapped inside a gated residential community that had narrow, winding roads and steep hills. Silencing myself had been a pattern I knew well, and while I hoped I would leave many of the unhealthy patterns that kept me far away from my Essence in Los Angeles, they had found their way into our home on wheels.

Jeremy focused on the navigation app, his eyes darting from his phone to the street in front of us. He swung Andi right, then left. No matter which way we drove, we couldn't exit, having driven into a giant maze with no apparent way out for a vehicle of Andi's size. Andi was as big as a semi, and so we had avoided underpasses that were under 13 feet, 2 inches tall. Often, I held my breath as we drove under and over bridges and through tunnels. We even had to make sure that Andi could fit under gas pump canopies, which was why we most often stopped for diesel at truck stops.

We were essentially a semi pulling a Jeep. And despite Jeremy's best effort to keep Andi out of this kind of trouble, we were stuck.

As I looked out the passenger window at the cars parked in the driveway of the house where we had stopped, they looked like toys. So small.

Making a U-turn was impossible, and backing up would most likely bend or possibly break the tow bar that connected the motorhome to the Jeep or jackknife Andi and the Jeep. Even driving forward on these kinds of streets put us at risk for running a curb, which could damage a tire or bend the rim. All this would be expensive to fix, and as we had learned, repairs cost time as much as money, if they could even be fixed at all.

Low-hanging branches scraped the roof as we inched forward, Jeremy craning his neck out the driver's side window to get a better view of the steep hill just ahead on the right. It appeared to be the only way out, but could he make the sharp turn and brake? I flashed to the runaway truck ramps I had seen on freeways, clenching my jaw, scrounging through my purse for lip gloss as a distraction. I wondered, smacking my lips together, where did the road even lead? Would it take us out of the community and back onto the main road? The knots began to tighten in my stomach as I weighed up the benefit of suggesting we unhitch the Jeep and drive it out or just letting Jeremy continue to problem solve. I hated this feeling of not being in control.

Since I had spent most of my childhood constantly masterminding ways to become the favorite child, I was adept at problem-solving, at figuring things out. Between not knowing what to do and how to solve it, plus trying to keep myself silent made me feel as trapped as Andi was. And as I watched Jeremy rotate his phone as he tried to find out where we were on the map app, as the weeks had turned into months living on the road, I realized living in an RV full time was not going to be the relationship fix I had been imagining. I had hoped that if we changed our lifestyle completely and left Los Angeles, where he had been so unhappy waiting it out until the kids were grown, that maybe he would be happy. But what was even more astonishing was that I hadn't even realized underneath all the adventure and excitement, as well as the fear of change I had been struggling with, a deeper issue had been hiding—the fact I had been hoping for years I could somehow engineer the perfect situation that could waylay all the struggles that made my husband frustrated, short-tempered, and a glass-half-empty kind of guy. Ultimately, the silence became too loud in the cockpit. I was too afraid of what it all might mean.

"Let's call the campground host and ask if he knows if this road will lead us out of here," I said, finally. "Or"—I paused, tearing at what was left of my cuticles—"what about unhooking the Jeep?"

Jeremy took off the baseball cap he had been wearing for days, smoothed back his thick graying hair, and placed the cap back on his head as he considered what I had said. I knew he had been e-mailing back and forth with the camp host for weeks, and as the campground was privately owned, I thought the guy would be friendly and maybe he could help. All I knew was that the navigation app was proving worthless, and we were both tired and hungry. And, worse than that, I felt myself on the verge of turning into a complete bitch.

Twenty minutes later, Jeremy had made the phone call to Tom, the camp host, but only after I had reapplied lip gloss half a dozen times and finished the bag of pistachios while Fergus sat perched on the dashboard, wondering if we were going to move or not. Simon moved from behind the recliner to a spot near the passenger seat where I could easily pet him. Before too long, a middle-aged man pulled up, smiling from the driver's seat of his blue Ford pickup truck. After assessing the situation, Tom and Jeremy decided it was best to unhook the Jeep and have me drive it out, following behind Andi.

Quickly, Jeremy jumped down out of his seat, scrambling to unhook the Jeep as fast as he could while Tom began to reverse his truck so he could lead us down the hill. I grabbed my backpack, taking the keys to the car and positioned myself in the driver's side of the Jeep to follow Andi down the hill. And within minutes, we were a happy convoy of three, slowly making our way down the steep neighborhood road and out onto the open freeway.

And just like that, within minutes, we were headed back to the motorcoach resort.

The next morning, I drank my coffee and sat outside near the fire pit as the breezes blew gently through our campsite. Deer grazed nearby, the spectacular views of the Sierra Blanca and Sacramento Mountain Ranges a lush blanket of greens and browns, enveloping me inside the tiny resort that was our home for the week. The fresh mountain air and tranquil wooded setting had erased the bitter taste in my mouth of the two days of travel, just like the vanilla creamer did to the instant coffee I now sipped. And so it went. We spent the next five days mesmerized by the deer in the morning and the bright-orange sun setting at night over the valley. I felt something like stability begin to take root inside me, lulled by nature. Even Fergus, the cheeky ginger cat who had learned how to open the screen door of the coach by himself, seemed lured by the sweet peace of this little corner of bliss. But I knew I was avoiding a truth.

Days later, when we were in Santa Fe, the nearby mountains recently having been consumed by fire that had left the entire city choking from the dirt and dust that filled the air and the rain falling for days as the dust turned to mud, I felt trapped inside Andi again. And within days, my anxiety returned. Maybe, I thought, it's because I missed being surrounded by nature. Maybe it was because I needed less desert and more greenery. I tried to focus more on noticing what I was noticing rather than trying to search for answers, so I stuck to my routine, spent extra time in meditation, and took lots of laps through the campsite, walking the surrounding trail.

I had experienced moments of simplicity in Ruidoso, and that did feel good. That simplicity felt like freedom, like resonance. Stability plus resonance equals simplicity, I thought. But the stability I had been relying on had been external. In order to feel stability, I had to be honest with myself.

Just because we were living in an RV did not mean that I was free from anything. It didn't mean that I would stop making U-turns in my life, constantly ending up stuck in exactly the same place. I knew true freedom would be to not *need* to be free from anything, that I would find freedom in turning toward my fears and being all of who I am, despite the consequence. There were still many truths I needed to face. I had to be brave. If I didn't address the issues in my relationship with Jeremy and things in my business, what I had been avoiding would continue to follow me wherever I went. And all of it was wrapped into pieces of my past that still needed resolution.

This was the truth I had been searching for. Owning less or living in a smaller space did not equate to the kind of simplicity I had hoped would erase the challenges I had been having. In fact, nearly every single thing about living in Andi seemed to complicate everything, as if instead of dragging the Jeep behind us, I had been hauling with me the truths I had not wanted to face. I wondered, had the entire idea to embark on the Radical Living Challenge been a mistake?

But this time, before I went into a complete state of panic, I thought back to the definition of simplicity: being in deep resonance with my Essence that was *untethered to the external circumstances around me.* This was the piece that I had to face so I could stop driving down the same one-way roads in my life, expecting to get to a different destination. It was time to acknowledge the truth. The freedom I needed to find was giving myself permission to see what was right in front of me.

I was stuck, and I had been lying to myself.

I hated the answer as much as I felt the resonance of truth wash over me like the breezes I had relished so much in Ruidoso. This was me, committing to radical honesty.

Now What?

In the process of getting to your truth, like me, you might experience:

Shame. The message you hear is usually in the voice of the Alligator telling you that you are bad, not worthy or enough, or not lovable at the core. For example, when I was younger, I believed that because I was not the favorite child, I was inherently bad or not good enough. And as a result, I had to develop coping mechanisms, such as making others' needs more important than mine, as a way to get love.

Unhealthy guilt. In this scenario, you beat yourself up relentlessly for mistakes or choices you make. You jump into regret or experience remorse. You may replay events in your mind over again, wishing you had done things differently. You might also become defensive or turn toward blame. You forget all about self-compassion. And, when this happens, you don't ask yourself Wisdom-Seeking Questions that might propel you forward in learning from the situation. If I had not explored radical honesty in Santa Fe, I might have continued to feel like I had for most of our relationship: that I alone could somehow perfect a lifestyle in which the patterns we had would disappear. I would have still believed this: "I should have never agreed to the Challenge. It's my fault that Jeremy and I aren't happy yet."

The other possibility is that you feel healthy guilt. When something you do or don't do feels dissonant, you can reflect and realize it is possible to make a more resonant choice next time. Healthy guilt teaches you we are always doing the best we can, and that the objective is to learn and grow and make different choices in the future. For example, I realized that there are new beliefs and behaviors I need to begin exploring to heal what is not aligned, believing, "I feel guilty I didn't know this earlier and didn't figure it out before getting on the road. Now that I know what I know, I can start healing what I have uncovered." When you are living life according to the Seven Questions, you understand that it is in your quest to express more of your Essential Self in this lifetime. You will fall down and make mistakes, and you can adjust as you go.

Let me be perfectly clear: the third question does not require you to be perfect. Rather, it asks you to begin to understand what it means to be honest. To strive for integrity, faithfulness, and honesty to yourself. To listen for resonance and dissonance and to remember that wherever you go, the truth will assert itself in some way or another. And this question asks you to act accordingly to untangle the knots and rewire and rewrite the life narrative written and directed by your limiting beliefs. It asks you to choose courage over comfort. It reminds you not to hide from the truth. It requires you to no longer be in avoidance, putting off or shoving things underneath the rug, afraid it will result in pain or discomfort. That you won't get what you want or will get what you don't want. Radical honesty asks you to be brave and address what is not aligned in your life.

However, that is not often easy to do. We get caught up in worry and fear.

And so, it is in the arena of radical self-honesty that most of us fall down, including me. This happens when you discover you have been settling for less or avoiding the longing or desire you have for something different. When you are not unhappy, but also are not happy, you must take heed of the voice inside.

When we consistently put the needs of others first or are in judgment of ourselves for what we truly want or need, we fall out of integrity with self. The question also asks you to be faithful to your dreams and, as a result, to the relationship you are building with yourself.

This third question asks if you can be trusted to be honest with yourself so that you can continue to learn and grow as the challenges of living a designed life are thrust upon us.

And of course, when we struggle or feel anxious or feel uncertain as we walk through the entangled knots of our lives, our feelings make perfect sense. Remember, your Alligator wants you to stay the same: safe and stuck in the little cozy condominium of perceived safety. This is a place in which you endlessly try to convince yourself that while you may be experiencing pain and longing for something more fulfilling in your life, it is *less* painful than the discomfort that comes from making big moves. Of risking what is safe. Of stepping outside your comfort zone. However, this is 100 percent a Big. Fat. Lie.

Let me tell you why.

Because, my friend, you are not being honest with yourself.

You are settling for what I call the *backup life*. When you are abiding by a code of radical honesty, you understand that self-responsibility is at the heart of everything we do. And while I know you may take 100 percent responsibility for saving for retirement, meeting performance goals at work, putting your kids through college, or making sure your parents are taken care of in their old age, to live life on your terms and get what you *really* want, you must also take responsibility for your commitment to having a life in which your Essential Self is fully expressed.

You must commit to you.

You must take a stand for your dreams and ideas. You must speak your truth.

You must make a vow to honor the relationship you have with your Essential Self.

Now, you may be saying that you are not sure you want to see what has been behind the proverbial refrigerator that is your life. I mean, there is stuff there that you just don't want to look at.

But you have made it this far. You can do this. Let's start with a baby step. Maybe just open one eye when you read this part.

Here's what the backup life looks like:

- When you are living it up in the backup life, you believe the Alligator. In fact, the Alligator is directing the version of your life where you are settling for the backup life. It says, "Maybe I wasn't meant to be in a relationship. I can accept that if I have to." Or "I can't be a single mom by choice. People will judge me." Or

"Only ten more years until I retire; it's not that bad, really. I can wait to do what makes me happy then." What does your Alligator say?

- You settle for good enough. Even if you tell yourself you're a person who would never settle, when you are not honest and rationalize or just power through the things in your life you are not energetically in flow or engaged with, you are settling. Whether it is for the extra weight you carry around or the wrong job, town, romantic partner, career, school, or friends, you *are* settling.

- When you feel as if you are just an arm's-length away from peace, joy, or contentment, waiting for an external result to make you feel better or wishing that the life you have is the life you want but knowing it isn't what you truly really desire—*that* is a backup life.

I'm challenging you to hear the truth.

It's time to stop thinking it will get better by itself. Stop pretending that the life you have in which you numb out with what we call *weapons of mass distraction*, like work or exercise or people-pleasing or wine or food or fixing or scrolling for hours on social media or whatever it is that allows you to believe the story you tell yourself that you are working on it or will work on it when the time is right—*that is living a backup life.*

The truth is, in all the scenarios, when you are not radically honest, you are choosing the backup life one decision at a time—moment to moment—and then that becomes your life. And, let's be honest: it's probably been this way for longer than you care to acknowledge. So, if you continue to hide from the truth, you will never get to fully express what you are meant to be and never have the life you know you were meant to live.

The challenge then becomes recognizing the voice of our consciousness, that of the truth.

The Two-Minute Radical Honesty Hack You Can Use Immediately

The Four-Way Check

One of the most powerful ways to listen to the truth is to create a stillness practice that encourages you to listen to different parts of yourself. Adapted from a process taught to me by the Hoffman Institute, as well as the Institute for Professional Excellence in Coaching (IPEC), you can use a tool we call the Four-Way Check. In this process, we will sit in stillness and seek honest feedback from:

- Our physical self
- Our emotions
- Our mind
- Our Essence

In this practice, we seek to listen to and meet our needs by cueing into what we are specifically holding inside ourselves somatically, through our body. Here is how you do it:

Either with your feet on the floor, sitting up, or lying down, close your eyes and bring your attention to your breathing. First, see if you can identify any way in which your Ghost is trying to assert itself into your consciousness. What is it saying or doing? Remind it that your Essence is leading for now and ask it to step aside.

Then, connect to the part of you that you identify as your mind (head) and engage in a dialogue. You can start by asking your mind, What's going on in there right now? What are you thinking about? Do you have any messages for me, Mind?

Then ask, What do you need right now to feel safe and calm? If your mind wants to go on and on with a list, then let it know you appreciate it but are moving on. You can also pause here, if you need to, and write down anything that is coming up that your mind wants you to hold on to.

Then, connect to your emotions. I think of this piece as connecting to my heart space. Now, ask your heart, What are you feeling, Emotions? What do you need? Listen with an open heart and compassion for yourself. Allow whatever feelings you have to arise without judgment. Be curious and open. Then, ask your heart what it needs right now to feel safe.

Next, you will connect to your physical self. Do a light scan of your entire body. What are you noticing? What sensations do you feel? Maybe there is tightness or muscle pain? Maybe you are hungry or feel bloated. Without judgment, just notice what is happening in your body. Then ask, What message do you have for me right now, Body? Your body message may come via sensation or words or images. Then, ask, *What do you need?*

Finally, connect to your Essential Self, the part of you that is the essence of what you truly are. Sometimes clients experience this sensation of self as just above them, in front of them, or within. Remember, this is the part of you that is pure and wise. Intuitive. She is in direct connection with the Divine. If it helps, imagine that you see her in all her beauty and radiance. Then ask, What message do you have for me, Essential Self? Listen and receive that message any way it comes to you! It may come in images, colors, or a feeling, or it might be the soft, still voice whispering to you gently. Ask this part of you what it might need to feel in resonance. Practice listening to the wise voice within that is your soul.

Last, celebrate yourself. Put all your attention on your heart space and then on the top of your head, allowing it to soften and receive energy from the Divine. Allow this loving light to pour down through you, filling every muscle, every organ, and every cell. Feel the oneness all the way down to the bottoms of your feet and all the way out to the edges of your skin. Bathe yourself in love and celebration. You are capable and clear. You are love.

RADICAL LIVING CHALLENGE:

Answer this question in your journal: What is one thing you need to get honest about now?

"The honest relationship you have with yourself will be a reflection of the peace you feel in your life."

CHAPTER 10

Reconnecting to Your OG Self

Pagosa Springs, Colorado

By now you have an idea of a few key concepts. And, since this is the part in the process where clients get lost in all those Wisdom-Seeking Questions and time tracking and radical honesty, we will review it all later in this chapter to make sure we are all literally on the same page. And, if you have not done the Time Tracking exercise or the What, How, and Why exercise completely, don't fear. I am also going to give you a hack that can help you continue through the process until you have time to complete your Time Tracking and the What, How, and Why exercises.

Now Let's Dive Back into Question 3

When I was seven, I went to a sleepaway camp called Camp Hitaga for the first time. I have a distinct memory of sitting at the wrought-iron kitchen table in our Iowa home, watching my mom, enamored, as what seemed like hundreds of white sew-in name labels floated down like snowflakes onto the table as she shook out the contents of the box that had been addressed to me. Her tiny wrists looked like those of a marionette as she shook it, grinning as she put the box down. Her short dark curls bobbed. Her straight white teeth, olive skin, and the warmth of her strong hands and thick fingers set on my back as she explained how she would sew each one of those little labels into the clothes she would pack into my suitcase for what would be my very first week away from home at camp.

The small girls-only camp was located about 30 miles from my hometown in Iowa, and I went each summer from the ages of 7 to 13. That first summer, wrapping my gangly arms tightly around scraped knees, I would sit on a log gathered around the campfire, singing at the top of my lungs alongside all the campers in my unit. I fell fast asleep, tucked into the top bunk inside my sleeping bag in a big cabin with glass windows, and woke to the sound of a trumpet. I spent my days and nights listening to the sounds of crickets and birds, learning how to make cheesy eggy potatoes on a skillet over a campfire, ricocheting like a pinball from horseback riding and swimming and archery to the arts and crafts cabin where I would perfect my skills weaving brightly colored yarns between the sticks I had found to make a God's Eye.

And when my parents drove the 60 minutes to pick me up at the end of that first week, I didn't have to do much begging to get them to let me come back for just one more week at camp. That first summer I extended six times, becoming part of the scenery. I returned to Camp Hitaga the following six summers, learning how to tie knots, properly fold the American flag, and canoe down the Wapsipinicon River. One summer, I slept in a tent built on a wooden platform and learned even more advanced outdoor living skills. I spent another in a covered wagon, living the lifestyle of a pioneer, and the summer before I turned 14, I slept in a tree-house with 8 other girls, and I spent most of my time in the stable, riding and caring for the horses. Each summer, my parents dutifully dropped me off on Sunday and picked me up on the following Saturday afternoon. My mom would do laundry, shake out my sleeping bag, and replace any of the labels that had somehow disappeared from my socks or T-shirts. Then, on Sunday morning, we would load up the car again and drive back to camp.

I forgot about camp and outdoor living the minute I hit puberty and discovered boys. That summer in the treehouse would be my last at camp.

I had not thought of that camping trip or Camp Hitaga for years until Jeremy and I arrived in Pagosa Springs, Colorado. When I was in my 20s and married to my first husband, his brother, Nick, an Outward Bound instructor, had taken us on a 10-day camping trip here. The three of us and Nick's dog, Rebel, hiked into the national forest with only a trail map and a compass, each of us carrying packs on our backs, two tents, and several heavy jugs of water. When I went on that camping trip, we hiked miles and miles of switchbacks through the mountains that week, and I felt strong and capable. I used the campfire cooking skills I had learned at Camp Hitaga each morning and night. When we completed that hike, dirty and without seeing any other humans for days, I felt invincible. And as I had walked out of the tall trees into a vast meadow on the way back to the parking lot where we had left our car, my senses came alive as I feasted on the sight of wildflowers, heard birds, and felt the sensation of my tall, strong body navigating through the wilderness. I knew somehow that feeling inside me felt like home. The same soul that had felt so aligned and at home during those days of summer camp.

Now here I was, 30 years later, back in Pagosa Springs. Andi was tucked into a perfect spot at the Wolf Creek Run Motorcoach Resort, just 35 miles north of the New Mexico border. Set underneath two enormous trees that were also the home to what seemed like hundreds of birds, I woke one morning to find the Katz Brothers titillated, tiptoeing back and forth and back on the wide dashboard, their necks craning upward into the trees. As the birds chattered and chirped, the cats' tails quivered at the sight of all those flying creatures in one place. Grabbing my hot mug of coffee, I decided to venture out to see the birds and possibly meditate on one of the benches overlooking the San Juan River.

The rain had finally stopped, and it looked like bits of dandelion fluff had been blown across the horizon by angels. As it was early summer, the river was high, and it hummed, churning over and through the rocks that jutted out everywhere. The shrubs and trees that lined the river were in all shades of green, and the dirt that had recently become mud from all the rain glistened in the sun. Sitting there, it felt like even my skin was more alive than it had ever been. I took in the scene, in awe this was just a regular Sunday on the road. As I closed my eyes and listened to the river run and the birds twittering, memories of Camp Hitaga and that camping trip I had taken almost 30 years before in this same mountain range flooded back to me, and I felt that same sense of *home*.

It all made sense. I had rediscovered a part of my Essential Self that had been buried for years. The part of me that had loved being at camp, that had felt so enlivened during the camping trip in my twenties. I thought back to the few times when I was single that I had taken my daughters camping at Sequoia National Park, teaching them how to set up a tent, build a decent campfire, and make cheesy eggy potatoes on it.

Sitting on that bench near the river, I felt connected to Essence, to nature, and to the need for adventure that was part of my DNA. I felt the same oneness with soul and Universe I had experienced as a child and in my twenties as a young mom but hadn't known what it was. This was what I had been craving all along but had not known it until this very moment. And as I sat on that bench listening to the river flow, I knew this feeling was my natural state of being. I took a sip of hot coffee, opening my eyes wide and taking it all in, feeling immense gratitude at having recognized myself again for the first time in decades. I had forgotten this part of myself. I had never even considered the connection I had to nature might have been factory installed.

What Is Lost Can Be Found

Sometimes when you get lost in the sauce of becoming what you think you are *supposed* to be, you lose parts of yourself. Conditioned by parents, teachers, mentors, and social media, you might compare yourself to everyone, forgetting what it is that makes your skin feel alive. The part of you that is uniquely you, the part that wants to be expressed in your life now. But you find that you are letting life live you instead of you living your aligned life.

However, now that you are beginning to define the key qualities of your Essential Self, you too can begin to refine and add to your list of qualities by revisiting your own childhood and young adult memories to see if parts of you have also become dormant in the pursuit of achieving and simply surviving. Often, even though you are working on yourself through therapy or meditation or attending weekend workshops, you forget what you truly are. You work so hard to unburden your hurts and remove negative ways of being and thinking that you forget to ask what inside you *is* essential? What is, in fact, the Essence of what and who we are?

We're Halfway There!

So, let's recap before we go further.

In Chapter 8, you started to define your Essential Self. And after reviewing your time tracking, you created a list of:

WHAT you enjoy doing

How best you enjoy carrying out the WHAT and the HOW

And the CORE MOTIVATION—your WHY—that makes it all feel aligned

Ultimately, you are going to use the list you are cultivating to design your life in upcoming chapters, creating ways for you to express your Essential Self in day-to-day life more often than not.

Here is an example of the list I created from this exercise that even at the time of the writing of this book still captures my Essential Self. I'm sharing it here now so you can continue thinking about your list and as a reminder to go back at any time during the process to adjust it based on what you are noticing about yourself.

What I enjoy:

Sitting around with people I enjoy, talking
Learning
Teaching
Creating something
Dinners and talking around the table afterward
Exercise

Working toward a goal
New experiences
Deep conversations
Music

Here's my How:

Small groups 1:1
Slow
Sitting in community
Sharing myself
Nature
Novel
Off the beaten path
Creative

And my Why:

Helping people
Entertaining
Caring for, nurturing
Health and well-being
Challenging
Fills up my need for curiosity
Exploring
Evolution of my best self
Bringing people together
Creating new things
Fun and play
Researching
Playing games
Travel

Chapter 9 offered strategies like the Four-Way Check to keep you radically honest with yourself as a way to practice what you have been learning in the study of question 2—a great tool to help you to continue to authentically be *you*.

Can you see how it is all starting to fit together?

I know you might be thinking, "I'm not sure I have the time to do all this four-way checking, Marni." Or maybe you did it for a few days but got too busy to be consistent. Or maybe you fell behind and still haven't completed your time tracking. Or maybe you are even feeling a little better having surfaced the Essential Problem, and now that your eyes are open, you have made some changes. Perhaps you are even thinking that maybe you aren't living the backup life after all.

Here's the thing: you don't have to perfectly use the questions and tools we have been discussing to start to create your next chapter and be living life on your terms.

Radical Living isn't about doing it perfectly. It's about doing life with intentionality. And doing it on your own terms. In fact, if you are feeling short on time or feel like even taking baby steps feels too hard right now, I highly recommend taking this shortcut to help you get honest and get back to being you.

It involves a very simple Wisdom-Seeking Question: It's a strategy called, Stop. Breathe. Ask. Or SBA for short.

It's really simple because it just asks you to recognize that the nagging, critical voice in your head is the Alligator.

It asks that you stop what you're doing in order to stop your negative thoughts. Then take a giant inhale, followed by a long, slow exhale. (This is the BREATHE part.)

Then, ASK yourself the simplest Wisdom-Seeking Question ever: What's *really* going on here? This question allows you to take a beat and get honest with yourself.

Is the thought you are having a limiting belief?

Or are you assuming that something bad will happen because it happened in the past?

Or maybe you just want the Alligator voice to shut up once and for all so you can connect to your grown-ass adult self.

Even if you get off track and feel like you barely have three minutes to attend to the work of creating your meaningful life or find yourself in the middle of chaos, SBA allows you to stay honest and keep grounding yourself back to the authentic you by asking the very simple Wisdom-Seeking Question, What is *really* going on here?

Defining Your Essential Self Today:
What, How, and Why

Review the list you are creating of key qualities that define your Essential Self. Keep in mind, however, that you are not meant to have a final answer in this exploration of Essence. This is not a quiz show, and you will not win a million dollars if you get it right. In fact, this Soul Map—this definition of self—will evolve over the course of your lifetime as you iterate and evolve through the Life Design process. And as I have said before, the exercises and questions within each chapter are yours to revisit at any time. As you may have already experienced through the exercises you have already completed, the more you dive into them, the more opportunities there are to take a second or third pass on an exercise and learn more.

Finally, as you develop your understanding of your Essential Self, when you more deeply tap into what are the essential threads within you, you will more deeply unlock the feeling state and vibrational energy of what is typically described as meaning or fulfillment—and that is what we are going for. We want to feel like we are living life rather than letting life live us, stuck in the boring middle. We want to have more moments like I had near the river in our daily life.

Taking It Deeper

Here is the hack if you don't have that list of qualities of your Essential Self. And for those of you who have the list, get ready to go a bit deeper.

Look back at your life from a place of curiosity and notice if there are any dots in your past experiences that you can connect. Patterns, threads, or pieces that seem to repeat that might define you being *you*. Think of those experiences as moments that illustrate or capture further the energy of what you are, as if it were an energetic thread flowing through you and out into the world as an expression of *you*—an active energy that's part of who you are when you are being you. In my own experience of doing this exercise, I realized while skimming through the peak experiences of my life as a child and young woman that connection to the outdoors was a theme, and I also noticed these experiences were not exclusive to moments I had as an adult on trips with my family and husband. But rather, I had this part of me inside, but it had been dormant. Perhaps this process will confirm what you have already recognized in the What, How, and Why exercise or help you to more strongly identify with a part of you that you have begun to uncover in this process.

For me, I discovered that when I am engaging in Radical Living, I am more often than not being the Essence of me, and that feels like freedom. For me, freedom feels like space in the middle of the quiet. There is no needing, there is no judgment, and there are no *shoulds*. It feels like a beautiful place of peace and self-acceptance, of being in surrender. Freedom for me feels like not needing to be, or do, for love or acceptance. It feels like trust and faith in the Universe, in the Divine. Freedom feels like a place where it feels safe to be courageous. Freedom is in the past not impacting the present. Freedom is the place of possibility. Freedom is presence. Freedom is the ability to experience what is resonant and follow that resonance. In this journey, I describe it as "what blows my hair back." And sitting there on that bench next to the river, connected to freedom, felt like softness and grace. And when you are in freedom, you can focus your consciousness on what is your birth state, a state that is one of love, peace, and contentment.

What freedom feels like to you can be anything from a cinematic experience to being unburdened by the past.

Now it's time to continue developing your understanding of your Essence and begin defining what freedom means to you. Using the knowledge and wisdom you have gathered, what does it mean to be free?

RADICAL LIVING CHALLENGE:

Part 1: Now that you have your What, How, and Why, can you take it even deeper by looking at the patterns, threads, and dots you connected from your ideal day exercise that further define characteristics of your Essential Self? Rewrite the list of characteristics that are *you* and continue to explore ways to connect and live from this place of authenticity on a daily basis.

Part 2: Now, since most of us desire Freedom, let's talk about how we create it and how it is connected to your Essential Self. Keep in mind the reason we do this work is so you can begin to connect to the feeling state or sense of aliveness and fulfillment that feels like Freedom. To begin, answer the following questions in your journal: Where in your life do you experience the feeling of freedom? Or where did you experience it long ago? What does freedom feel like in your body? Remember, it might not be words that define this for you; it might be felt senses or memories. Consider what freedom feels like in context of your inner state as well as your relationships: romantic, familial, and professional. What are the experiences you have had that light you up, that blow your hair back? What does a lack of freedom feel like? Define freedom as a way of being. What are you doing, thinking, and feeling when you are embodying freedom?

Above all, freedom is not needing to be free from anything. So, as you explore and study this concept, create, and define freedom for yourself. Remember it is your birthright to be free once again.

> "Set yourself free in your own mind
> about what is possible."

CHAPTER 11

With the Right Question, the Truth Can Be Uncovered

The Million Dollar Highway, Ouray, Colorado

With a deep crush on Colorado beginning to form, Jeremy and I headed off toward Ouray via what is known as the Million Dollar Highway, a stretch of road running through a gorge that is characterized by steep cliffs, hairpin S curves that cut directly into the mountains, and a mind-blowing lack of guardrails. I was terrified of the drive, but I knew that if I focused on being videographer, Jeremy could put his attention on driving rather than capturing the epic feat we were about to attempt on video. With both hands firmly on the wheel, Jeremy maneuvered Andi steadily, as awed by her capability as the potential for disaster. I reminded him to keep his eyes ahead and sat with my shoulders pointed straight ahead, my back rigid, while holding the GoPro out the window.

Jeremy drove Andi as if riding a thoroughbred, intuition as important as skill. We had discussed that Andi's brakes were already hot from coming through Durango and the long list of other mountain towns we had driven through, and Jeremy wanted to make sure we slowed down to the recommended speed before making the descent into Ouray. He knew that if he started Andi in too high of gear, or out of gear, he would have to push harder and harder to brake, and the brakes would become less and less responsive with the same amount of pressure. And with that pressure, the brakes would continue to get hotter and hotter, transferring the heat to the drum, then to the rim, and then to the tires, risking a blowout or even the entire rig catching fire.

Again, I thought of runaway truck ramps and kept my eyes on the road ahead.

By the time we were fully into the descent, Jeremy used the engine brake to adeptly control our speed. As we drove sometimes at just 20 miles an hour, I remembered a phrase I had used with clients in reference to dating: "The slower you go, the faster you'll get there." That is, until we made the final turn into Ouray just one mile out of town.

Jeremy smelled burning rubber.

"Pull over, pull over!" I shouted, as the choking scent intensified in a matter of seconds. Jeremy furrowed his brow, checking the tire pressure gauge on the dash, looking in the rearview mirror for smoke as the smell inside the cabin intensified. I imagined flames engulfing the rig as the overwhelming smell of stinking burned tar filled Andi's interior cabin.

"Stop. Just stop! I need to focus." A clear command from the captain's chair indicating it was up to me to manage my terror silently. He had never been good at calming me down in the midst of a crisis; rather he narrowed his eyes on the road as if I were invisible, navigating yet another hairpin curve. Attempting to cool the brakes, he kept his foot off the brake for a few seconds at a time, reducing our speed from 20 miles per hour to 10 several times in a row. And as I looked for signs of smoke emanating from the tires, it was clear it was still taking too much time to reduce the speed than it was for gravity to increase it. And after almost 10 rounds of this approach, it was clear Jeremy had no more brakes. My heart racing, I closed my eyes.

That is, until time stopped, and the road seemed to magically level out just in time for Jeremy to steer Andi over into a pullout where we could stop and let the brakes cool off before continuing the descent into town.

I opened my eyes and let out a giant exhale, glancing out the right passenger side door to assess the situation. And there in the distance was Ouray, "the outdoor recreation capitol of Colorado."

I got out of the rig as if in a trance.

Jeremy scrambled from his seat in the captain's chair to join me outside as I stood, captivated, the line of wrinkles in my forehead crinkling into deep ridges as I drew my eyes upward, then down to the historic mountain town below, mouth open wide, like a bird waiting for a bit of food from its mother.

As we stood together on the shoulder of the road, we could only see the roofs of shops and houses and the famous hot springs below. All of it was encased within the rugged, jagged vertical walls of the 12,000- to 14,000-foot peaks of the looming San Juan Mountains. A box canyon indeed. As I took in the view, I imagined the lives going on inside this geographic bowl. Since there were no flames to worry about on the RV, I focused on the beauty right there in front of me.

Nothing else mattered. The cracks and crevices of the mountains, their peaks stretching into the clouds extended like the arms of a ballerina. I looked into the heavens, catching a flicker of sunlight reflecting off the water cascading onto the rocky ledges below, the water curling itself into the mountains as it fell, watching it, down, down, falling toward the town and river below, hitting the bullseye.

I thought then about the problems I had believed were the real problems that were in the way of me feeling peace and joy. I had been pretending the problems were burning rubber. Or driving an RV the size of a semi down a winding mountain road. RV repairs. Leaving LA. Or selling the house. The Alligator in my head being full of judgment, criticism, blame, and regret. Or Jeremy. So many problems I could be led to think were the *real* problems. The truth was these were external conditions, situations I wanted to fix and control. Yes, we did need to solve those problems, but the mistake would be to believe if I could solve them once and for all, joy, peace, and fulfillment could be mine. Then life would "blow my hair back."

"Fix it and be free." This had been my mantra. But I knew better now.

When I was radically honest, I saw the Essential Problem buried beneath the surface. And that was that I had attached that feeling of home to the house in LA, being a mom or a CEO, or achieving a certain level of success. This was the Essential Problem. I had relied on all those external things to keep me stable and anchored. And I had been terrified of change because I believed that if I moved one of the pieces in my life, everything might break apart, and I would be lost. However, the real problem I now faced was that without the footholds I had clung to, I had to learn how to find that sense of home inside me, regardless of circumstance. The journey of Radical Living was teaching me my Essential Self was inside me. And that this was the feeling of home I had been seeking all along. I had been mistaken in thinking peace or joy or happiness or even fulfillment came from those experiences that were outside me. Instead, the source of those feelings had been right there inside me all along. I just didn't know it was there. And that source was my Essential Self. My soul. Encased in my body. Like a box canyon.

Once You Surface the Essential Problem, You Are in a Choice Point

I had been here before. I remembered being married to my ex-husband and, as a young mother, how I had avoided the potentially unsettling and life-changing truth that I was miserable in my marriage. I remembered pushing it all away, pumping the brakes again and again, hoping to slow it all down and just figure out a way to be happy. I just wasn't ready. I was too afraid. I did not understand there was something beyond because I could only see what I knew.

And maybe you aren't sure if you want to surface the Essential Problem either. That's okay. I understand what it feels like. My mind had been closed too. In that moment in my late thirties, I was connected to a certain life, and that life had momentum. I was entrenched in that timeline. That life in which I was a young wife and mother, living in the house with the white picket fence.

And as such, there had been a lot of momentum carrying me forward into a future I had imagined for most of my life up until that point.

And now as a result of being human, the same thing had happened again when I married Jeremy and became entrenched in the momentum of my life in Los Angeles, feeling like I was spinning and spinning, cartwheeling through space and time, unable to stop the momentum of the life I was familiar with, even if I knew something was not quite right.

That is what I call a Momentum Tunnel.

In both these times of my life, after much kicking and screaming, I ultimately made a new choice. I surfaced the Essential Problem: that I wanted to be even more deeply aligned and authentic. I stalled the momentum of that timeline and that life so I could course correct and redirect in a new, more aligned Momentum Tunnel.

I knew then that just as Jeremy had to bring Andi to a complete stop so that we could see the beauty as well as face the fear of what might be lost, the discomfort of the liminal space was just me breaking the momentum of the life I had left behind. It wasn't going to be a one and done.

I had to continue to open myself to curiosity and willingness to surface new versions of the *real* problem.

The Problem You Think You Have Is Not the Real Problem

Let's recap:

As we begin to complete our study of question 3, there is much to celebrate. You have identified the qualities of your Essential Self and are beginning to see patterns to what blows your hair back! Plus, you have become adept at asking Wisdom-Seeking Questions to untangle the knots that allow your Essential Self to surface more as you experience life.

In this chapter, you will take the next step and identify the *real* reason why you have not been able to live the life that truly blows your hair back. The one truth that has probably been hiding just below the surface—underneath all that rationalizing and generally avoiding feelings, situations, and beliefs that are painful—where you can't see it in the subconscious. This one truth will most likely be the reason why you never started that side business. Took that trip. Broke up with that guy. Or committed to the person you have been dating for years. Or maybe it's the reason why you stayed in that job where you aren't respected or aren't making the money you deserve. Or, why no matter how hard you try, you are never able to keep off the weight or start that exercise plan.

You know what I mean. It's the honest-to-goodness truth that up until now you haven't been able or willing to see.

Let's get started.

In this step, we will use good old Wisdom-Seeking Questions to help you surface the real problem that is keeping you stuck in the life that is good enough but not great. We call this problem your Essential Problem. Your Essential Problem is the one central thread that, when discovered and then handled, will enable you to live life like a ninja! You are stealth and less attracted to the chaos of life.

Surfacing the Essential Problem is like hitting the jackpot because when you do and address it head-on, so much of what has been keeping you stuck no longer makes sense.

However, there is a catch.

In order to surface the Essential Problem, you must be honest with yourself and others because often it is a problem you have been pretending not to know you have. My guess is every time it occurs to you that this is something you have to address, you shove it under the carpet and power through, letting life live you.

I'll let you sit with that a moment.

So, what you do to cope with the problem is compensate in other parts of your life. You create a narrative in which there is another problem. One you think can be solved with the next great hack, tip, technique, strategy, program, plan, or thing.

I had a client who consistently overscheduled herself and was exacerbating her frustration by asking external questions like, Why do I keep doing this stupid thing again and again? Well, as a result of all the stress and worry at work, she began steadily gaining weight and feeling exhausted. She had left her corporate job to build her own business, but as she put more and more focus on building it, it became harder to maintain her weight. For her, eating healthy food and exercising felt like another task on her list—an obligation—versus something that would help her have the vitality and well-being she envisioned for herself. And because she was worried and stressed so much of the time, she often turned to food as a reward.

She was determined not to give up, so she continued to power through, hoping she could out-think her problems. She tried different diets. She joined diet-related Facebook groups. She listened to podcasts and took supplements. She made rules about when to eat and what to eat. She even gave herself cheat days so she could reward herself with food as part of her routine. And when her clients needed to cancel at the last minute or asked her to meet unreasonable deadlines, she would work longer hours to accommodate their schedules. She was always understanding. Compliant. She was striving to make her clients happy at all costs. She wanted to be *good*. Then, when her partner lost his job because he had to care for his elderly parents, she rationalized again, believing it was acceptable for him to ignore her needs because he was under duress. My client easily put his needs first while forgetting her own, just like she had with her clients. She thought that setting boundaries, expressing anger, and advocating for herself was selfish. And the more she squashed her needs and desires, the more she felt she deserved to eat whatever she wanted to eat. All the diets and tricks she tried continued to fail, and she continued to gain weight.

This client was terrified to face the *Essential Problem*. She didn't want to give up the belief she had that making her needs as important as that of others was selfish. It wasn't until she began to work on question 3 and practiced radical honesty that she realized she believed putting the needs of her boyfriend and her clients first made her a "good" person. Something she had learned growing up.

Can you see how the problems she thought she had weren't really the Essential Problem? She didn't have a weight problem or a business problem or even a relationship problem.

As this client continued to ask Wisdom-Seeking Questions, she surfaced even deeper truths. Struggling with her weight felt like something she could, and therefore should, control. That felt like a familiar problem. One she could handle. However, since she knew she couldn't control how her partner or clients might respond if she set boundaries, she avoided the Essential Problem completely. Instead, she continued to focus on dieting and controlling food.

This is why I offer you this honesty question: *What is it that you're pretending not to know in order for you to have the problem you think you have?*

Think about it. Take a beat. Let it sink into you.

It's complicated, I get it. And that's the point. It's not a question you can answer easily with your mind. Sometimes clients hear this question and the answer hits them square in the middle of their chest. Like a punch. And sometimes clients simply default to their rational, problem-solving brain. When that happens, what often comes up are things like, "I don't get it." Or "I don't know." Both of which become the great cover-up for "I don't want to deal with it."

Whatever happens for you, understand that as you practice asking Wisdom-Seeking Questions, you will become more comfortable with the ideal of *allowing* the answer to come in a way and at a time that might surprise you.

As you consider this question, I recommend you not focus on what it means, per se, but rather allow your mind to untangle it and begin to journal. For example, your brain could unpack the question in a way that looks something like this:

What is it?

What is it that I'm pretending . . .

not to know . . .

in order to have the problem . . .

I think I have?

Ponder it. Go for a walk, holding the question in your mind. Allow it to unfurl and unwrap itself as the truth or truths become available for you. Give yourself permission to hear the truth and celebrate how courageous you are becoming.

Remember, when you surface the Essential Problem, you can begin to work on solving the actual pieces that will create a shift in your life rather than continuing to work harder at what won't work. Knowing the Essential Problem is the key to unlocking what is preventing you from living life on your terms.

So How Do You Get the Courage to Make a New Choice?

First, if you feel as uncertain as I did at certain parts of the journey, remember that in designing your Radical Living Challenge, you do not have to make choices that will blow up the life you have. You don't have to get a divorce or quit your job. Or move to a new town. The objective is to take one baby step at a time and let the process here do its thing, ultimately taking action based on where you feel comfortable either stalling the momentum slowly by taking small steps one at a time or stopping it altogether and making bigger changes that are suited to your goals and level of comfort.

Your courage, however, will come more easily in the face of question 4 when you learn to intentionally source that anchored and self-assured energy from within. In short, this means you can find the source of your worthiness, capabilities, genius, and truth internally. And that when you feel stuck or the Alligator is telling you its lies, you can come back to the real Source whenever you want.

Let me break it down in a way that is simpler to understand.

Remember when I shared that I had been making the external conditions in my life like my business or my house the source of my feeling of stability? Of peace and joy and fulfillment? The problem is that when we do it this way, it becomes exhausting. It creates overwhelm, burnout, and the feeling of never being satisfied. We don't feel enough or confident unless we win. And that's because we are looking for hits of the feel-good chemical dopamine in the things that happen to us. We source externally. For example, when you are dating and can't access that you are enough and lovable when you don't get asked on a second date. Or when you don't get the job. Or a promotion. Or close the deal. When you are not Re-Sourcing internally, all those things make you feel wobbly and uncertain.

And you can see how that actually makes you very unstable and resistant to change and trying new things.

To Re-Source is to plug into the felt sense of stability from within. It's being able to connect to Essence as the source of your power rather than needing an outlet that often isn't anywhere to be found, especially when it is outside of your control. When you can source stability, peace, joy, and fulfillment from within, however, you shift from needing external sources to feel confident, enough, and lovable to sourcing from Essence. When you Re-Source, it's like having access to a neon sign inside you connected to a magical never-ending source of electricity that is always flashing: I am capable. I am enough. I am safe. The Universe has my back.

And when you make this the reality you live in daily, you will naturally feel more ease and stability in your life and begin to make choices and have beliefs that are aligned with this way of feeling and being. For example, you can more easily set boundaries or say no to things that are part of the old way you lived your life. You are more courageous, saying yes to things that feel uncomfortable or messy because you are committed to being resonant with your Essential Self. You can more easily recognize knots and entanglements and work through them. You understand that the real problems are problems because you are not aligned or in integrity with the true authentic you, your Essential Self. And that means that you feel more empowered.

And once you get better and better at Re-Sourcing through practicing, you will slowly create new momentum until you begin to find yourself in a brand-new Momentum Tunnel. One step at a time.

You break the momentum of the old timeline and redesign a future in which you live a life that blows your hair back. You can more honestly look at the pieces of your identity and recognize which of those are dying. Which of those are no longer authentic. And what you can no longer tolerate because it is not aligned with your Essential Self.

Day by day, as you begin to Re-Source your confidence and magic from Essence within and connect into the qualities of what you truly are, you not only build momentum toward your new identity and future but also discover freedom. Spinning in this new Momentum Tunnel feels fun and exciting. You feel on fire! Like you can manifest anything. This means you are more firmly connecting to your Essence and beginning to make new choices and have new thoughts that are aligned.

Of Course, There Will Be Obstacles and Hurdles Along the Way

Even as you are trying to source deeper and deeper into more of your Essence and that blow-your-hair-back energy, it is normal to get caught up in the timeline of the life we are leaving behind. Re-Sourcing is not always easy. Especially when you first begin. You grasp for the materiality of life. The familiarity. The identity that you thought was going to bring meaning and fulfillment to your life yet isn't. Just like I experienced on the road, as you go through this process, there will be things in place that will try to force you back in the old direction and timeline.

That doesn't mean you are doing it wrong or that the Universe is telling you to stay where you are. Remember, the Alligator voice will get the loudest the closer you walk to the border of living life in a new way. Be gentle. Go back and revisit early chapters to focus on bringing more of what you love into your life in ways that align with your Essence using your What, How, and Why. Continue asking Wisdom-Seeking Questions. And remember the process is as important as the destination.

Even if you feel stuck or lost or aren't sure what your problem is, you can begin by noticing as you go through your days where you are sourcing your energy from. What could it look like to no longer source from ego or the craving side of the egoic mind? And as you begin to live courageously and face the problems you surface, remember the Seven Questions and the framework you are learning here will provide a deep well of comfort and power from which you can draw peace.

EXERCISE: GETTING CLARITY.
What Is the Momentum Tunnel You Want to Stall?

Using your findings from Chapters 1 through 10, ask yourself the following questions.

Surfacing Your Essential Problem

- **What are the problems and challenges in your current life?** Make a list of the problems and challenges you are experiencing now. Put them all down on paper and get them out of your head. If it makes you feel overwhelmed, that's okay because you are practicing radical honesty. The goal is not to solve them all right now; the purpose is to begin to see if you can connect the dots and discover what might be the real problem. Consider my client Andrea.

  Andrea wanted to retire soon from a corporate job she held for 30 years. She had been dating her boyfriend, Dave, for two years. She realized in doing this work that since most of her family no longer lived in the town where she lived, she wanted to relocate. Andrea initially believed her problem was choosing the right place to call home. However, in doing the exercises you are doing now, Andrea understood that she continued to avoid the situation because she worried about what Dave would think if she told him she wanted to move. She also wondered what her adult children might think. She even started second guessing the work she had done with her financial planner, wondering if she could retire at all. Above all, Andrea wondered what would happen if she made the wrong decision. Andrea surfaced the Essential Problem, however, when she connected the dots and realized she didn't trust herself to make decisions. Worrying about how her decision might impact others and whether she had the financial stability to retire were distractions from the real problem. But once she surfaced this problem, she internally began to source her confidence and identify what was right for her from Essence. She spoke to Dave about her concerns, as well as her children, and learned they supported her decision. She revisited the conversation she had with her financial planner. And ultimately, she knew she had the resources to retire when she planned. And then, Dave jumped into the process you are learning here with Andrea so that they could work toward that future timeline by creating new momentum together now for their next chapter together.

- Brainstorm a list. What might the *real problems* be that you have? Which is the one you feel most drawn to that might be important for you to address right now?

Now that you have an idea of an Essential Problem, where does the problem present itself most often? In what situation or contexts are you when you face these problems? Are there other people involved too? Are there any patterns or similarities that stem from your fears or uncertainties? Listen to the voice of the Alligators to help you see what beliefs you may need to release or shift in order to truly solve the Essential Problem.

Why is it important that this Essential Problem be solved? What is at stake if you do not live a life fully expressed from truth and Essence? How could not solving the Essential Problem hold you back?

If you are still not sure what your Essential Problem is, you have two options:

- Take a guess. Continue working through the process as if this is the Essential Problem. Continue to see wisdom and let the process reveal more to you as you go through it.

- Continue working through the book and the exercises, trusting that the Essential Problem will reveal itself to you as long as you continue asking Wisdom-Seeking Questions and are radically honest with yourself. You may want to continue to do the walking meditation in this chapter to create space and time to allow the wisdom to bubble up.

A Few Thoughts . . .

You might have a lot of problems going on at the same time. That's okay. The purpose of this exercise is to expose the truth about what is no longer working in your life. It's your time to try on radical honesty. Do not beat yourself up for what you surface. Remember to practice self-compassion, as it is a fundamental part of question 1. Sometimes this part is uncomfortable, which means you are most likely facing truths you have been previously avoiding. Congratulations!

RADICAL LIVING CHALLENGE:

Exercise: Write a futuristic story of your new Momentum Tunnel! Pretend you are looking back at the end of this process and describe the qualities of your Essential Self and tell the story of how you changed in the process of living a radical life on your terms. What did you have to leave behind in order to exit the old Momentum Tunnel? Why was it worth it? Describe your new future and the steps you took to become that future version of you, aligned with Essence more often than not.

"We don't want our wounded selves
to author the rest of our lives."

Question 4

04   Did You Busy Yourself with Creation?

In your time on Earth, you are asked: Were you busy planting seeds? It is not "did you leave behind money or possessions or even love?" It asks whether you invested in the being of what it is you hope to leave behind. What will you create that is lasting, that thing that will ripple through time and nurture those who come next?

Introduction to Question 4

You probably picked up this book because you have been defining success or meaning in your life through an accounting of your achievements. And that makes sense, since most humans have been taught to believe the sum value of a life should be defined in a way in which you measure its worthiness by asking if you left behind money or possessions, or even love.

However, as you have begun to discover, living a life in which we focus on doing, rather than being, will forever lead us down the path of never feeling satiated or enough. And as such, the fourth question shifts yet again how you go about creating a life of meaning by asking, Did you busy yourself with creation?

Before you tell me that you are not creative or talented, or that you don't know the first thing about creating post-worthy content on social media, the definition of *create* we are using here is to bring something new into existence that has zero to do with getting followers on Instagram, your talent, or even completing an art project. Instead, the fourth question more specifically asks: Have you invested in the being of what it is you hope to leave behind? What will you create that will ripple through time and nurture those who come next?

CHAPTER 12

You Can't Take It with You When You Go

Gros Ventre Campground, Grand Teton National Park

I set up my makeshift desk at what was also the kitchen table for a meeting with a client. So often the question I asked a client was one I had recently asked myself, and there had been many times since we had left the last campsite that this overlap had me considering the seeds I had been planting to start creating a sense of home inside me. I thought about how the journey thus far had led me to understand this may have been the ultimate destination after all. I sat down and waited for the notification that my client was waiting online and recognized that experiencing the physical sense of home inside me was a change in not only how I was living life but also different from the foundation on which I had built it.

Later that afternoon, I put the red harness and leash on Fergus to take him for a walk on a pathway that had been cleared for walking near the campsite. Chipmunks darted under fallen branches into the holes they had recently made or found, while Fergus put the weight of himself into his back paws and leaned forward, alert and ready to pounce as the sun began to drop in the Wyoming sky. I imagined his life as a simple housecat in LA and the foundation on which I had built that life—my house. It had represented security and the container where I discovered who I was as a divorcee, then a single mom, and ultimately as the woman in a relationship with Jeremy. It was the place where I had raised my three daughters, now independent and thriving on their own. I had established financial independence and established a blended family with two house cats who spent their days watching birds from a kitchen window. And how without realizing it, I had planted seeds that had flowered into a reliance on that house being the source of my sense of happiness and fulfillment. And even though that part of my life had ended, I had believed once again that this new 40-foot home, built on a chassis, might be the thing that would be the source of my joy.

But the journey itself and the questions thus far had pointed me to the truth. This was a time of planting seeds in brand-new soil, of creating something even deeper within me as the source of my meaningful life. Not the house in LA. Not Andi. Just me. Just as Fergus began to chitter and pull on the leash, seeking out the now-disappeared chipmunk, it was time for me to seek out the up-until-now hidden place inside me that would be a foundation on which to build the rest of my life. A place that was unwavering and resistant to whatever might happen outside of me, so different from the soil on which I had built my life before. A life that was no longer based on a set of rules and conditions imparted to me through social constructs over a lifetime that didn't align with a spiritual and meaningful life or even who I was at the core. And of course, all that had been impacted by taking on the roles and beliefs I had adopted from the experiences growing up in my family. All that chasing money, possessions, and even love. Believing the idea that some external thing or person or achievement would be the thing that would finally make me happy and therefore fulfilled.

But now I was determined to keep creating, planting seeds in new soil that would create a foundation that was strong, unflappable, and built solely on the qualities of my Essential Self, free from the Alligator voices, at least when I could remember to assert my powerful self over them. This was the real foundation that would defy change and chaos and provide long-lasting stability. A foundation for inner peace and joy as well as the ability to self-soothe and live from a place of strength.

Build with the Right Materials

Now, consider the foundation on which your house is built. If your very existence has been measured by how much money you make or leave behind, what material possessions you acquired, or even the loving relationships you have or don't have, the meaning of your life is going to be defined by results that are external and out of your control. And as we discussed in the last chapter, this creates instability in your life. In this mindset, you succeed or fail based on what you do or don't do and what you have or don't have.

Which sucks.

However, with this question, you get to build your house on a different kind of foundation. Rather than chasing the status and money and things you once believed would be the key to a meaningful life, you are redefining what it means to create. This question asks you to shift your focus from *doing* and *having* to *being*. The legacy you leave is not determined by what you have or what you leave to whom but rather how you *live your life*. Keep in mind that while the question refers to legacy, it is not limiting this to material things you might leave to your children or immediate family. In this context, legacy is something you create and leave, regardless of whether or not you have children that survive you.

In answering this question for yourself, you identify your own metrics of success. Living into this question is the key to absolute freedom.

I think of the word *create* like a three-legged stool. For our work here, let's examine this fourth question by looking at each of the three legs of creation.

What You Leave Behind

In its original form when the rabbis asked it, this question focused on legacy and procreation. However, what is important is the purpose behind the creation coming from a place of service, as being part of something bigger. In this case, you can think about this part of creation as contribution and being in service to that which you care about. It asks you to be intentional in what you do in the world. Not with the focus of creating financial security or your professional goals necessarily but with a higher purpose of making an impact in the world. To see beyond yourself in what you create. What will you leave as a mark of your Essential Self expressed in this world?

And remember, this might not have anything to do with work or purpose, as I said. Or your career. It is truly to create whatever it is you create from a place of service. And when you are in service or contribution, this creation brings joy and fulfillment. For some of you, it might happen at work. It might also happen in how you live and embody your values. The courage you display. Or your strength. Maybe you are a role model because of your sense of adventure or your humor or the way you care. I invite you to expand how you define service. One of the mantras I hold in this area of creation is to believe that service is joy and joy is service. They are one and the same. Interconnected. When we live a life of meaning and are in creation, there is a constant flow of both giving and receiving joy.

Being Intentional

The second tentacle of creation is that while creating can be associated with a certain skill or a certain talent, it is not limited to being "creative." Intention is the energy you bring to what it is you want to do, be, or have. The concept of "setting an intention" is not new. However, have you ever considered what that means, exactly? When you consciously Re-Source anabolic energy from within, through Essence, and direct it toward your goals, commitments, dreams, or anything that you are doing, you are consciously creating energy. The very act of having intention requires creative energy. And so it is through your conscious intent that you create. Slam dunk. Two points!

How You Create Your Life, Moment by Moment

The third tentacle of creation asks you to consider what you create moment by moment that will ripple through all time. I remember sitting in class as a new coach and watching a video featuring Bruce Schneider, my mentor and founder of the school I was attending. "Each moment gives you an opportunity to decide who you want to be in that moment," he said, his voice echoing through the TV monitor filling the room. I let that sink in. The stale air of that random hotel conference room in northern California suddenly became infused with possibility.

When you create, you are being in action of what is possible moment by moment. You are unequivocally free if you create from Essence. You are present in the moment when you create from the place of your deepest self. And when you listen to the knowing inside you, you also get the opportunity to create new thoughts, feelings, and actions that come from that space. When you consider how much power you have to create in all these ways, it is astounding. You are then responding to life from a place of your most whole self rather than from the hurts, traumas, and burdens of the past. Each day can become an unlimited source of your potential. And in this you have the possibility to create your life moment by moment—as part of your soul's evolution in this lifetime.

I know this feels like a lot. Is it even possible to be this actively engaged in creating your life?

The answer is that this creation question is not an ultimatum, nor is it something that we are either good or bad at doing. Rather, question 4 is here to support you when you feel hopeless. To help you remember you can create. When you are stuck or challenged, this question can be the lighthouse you can turn to when things feel dark, when you need to course correct and reorient yourself to the thoughts that can fill you up with the truth that you are enough and capable. Question 4 is here to remind you of the power you must choose.

Let's recap.

The only requirement is to create, beginning with the foundation that is your Essential Self. And from that place, creating is planting seeds.

To look beyond yourself and be in service.

To intentionally leave a piece of your soul behind.

To be the ripple that will last throughout time and nurture those who come next. To live moment by moment.

To intentionally live life on your terms, untangling the knots and attachments along the way.

RADICAL LIVING CHALLENGE:

As we have been challenging the very foundation on which you will begin to build a life lived on your terms, the exercises you will do in the following chapters will be the foundation to support you in beginning the process of designing your life and dreaming big.

Let's begin by getting clarity on your new identity based on your Essential Self. As you continue to tune in to your soul, this will become the foundation on which you will design your life.

Values are intrinsic to who you are; they are essences of your being. Some values will resonate with more energy for you than others because of who you are in your core.

Let's do some soul tuning. Sense your way into your core, your Essential Self. Reflect on your What, How, and Why, and select 10 values that you care about most.

Accountability

Accuracy

Achievement

Adaptability

Adventure/Discovery

Altruism

Ambition

Authenticity

Autonomy/ Independence

Awareness/ Consciousness

Balance

Beauty/Art/Harmony

Being the best

Belonging

Career

Caring

Choice

Collaboration/
Partnership

Commitment/Devotion

Compassion/Grace

Competence

Completion

Confidence

Contribution/Service

Cooperation

Courage/Boldness/
Fierceness

Creativity/Imagination

Dignity

Directness/Diversity/
Efficiency

Elegance/Refinement

Empathy/
Encouragement

Empowerment/Per-
sonal power

Environment

Equality Ethics

Excellence/Mastery

Excitement/Thrill/
Risk-taking

Faith Family/Friendship

Financial Stability

Forgiveness

Freedom

Friendship

Fun

Future generations

Generosity

Giving back

Grace

Gratitude

Growth/Learning/
Education

Harmony

Health/
Wellness/Fitness

Home

Honesty

Hope

Humility

Humor

Inclusion

Independence

Initiative

Innovation/Revolution

Integrity

Intimacy/Connection

Intuition

Job security

Joy/Fun

Justice

Kindness

Knowledge

Leadership

Learning

Legacy

Leisure

Listening/Reflection

Love

Loyalty

Making a difference

Nature/
Environmentalism

Nurturance

Openness

Optimism

Orderliness

Patriotism

Patience

Passion

Peace/Tranquility

Perseverance

Personal fulfillment

Power

Pride

Recognition

Resilience/Flexibility

Reliability

Respect

Resourcefulness

Responsibility

Risk-taking

Romance/Marriage

Safety

Security/Stability

Self-discipline

Self-expression

Self-respect

Sensuality/Sexuality

Serenity

Service

Simplicity

Spirituality/Faith

Sportsmanship

Stewardship

Success/
Achievement/Victory

Teamwork

Thrift

Time

Tradition

Travel

Trust

Truth

Understanding

Uniqueness

Usefulness

Vision

Vitality/Zest/Energy

Vulnerability

Wealth

Well-being

Whole-heartedness

Wisdom

Now, grab your journal and write down your top five values from the top 10 you have chosen.

Next, turn them into nouns (e.g., "creative" becomes "creativity").

Then, use your nouns to complete each of your "I am's" (e.g., "I am creativity.").

I AM _____

I AM _____

I AM _____

I AM _____

I AM _____

Finally, in your journal, describe in a few sentences who and what you are now based on the qualities you are identifying that are your Essential Self. Does this align with your What, How, and Why? Tune in to your Essential Self. What adjustments, if any, do you need to make as you continue to learn what is resonant? If you feel inspired, you can also include new beliefs you are beginning to adopt about what truly makes a life meaningful based on what you are learning. Reflect on the way you built your life and how it once served you but no longer will dictate what you create for the rest of your life.

> "The dance of resonance with your soul is like riding the moguls. Keep your skis pointed downhill and just enjoy the freakin' ride."

CHAPTER 13

Listening to the Whisper of Wings

Jackson, Wyoming

Even though it was the middle of summer and the national parks were packed with visitors, a few days later, Jeremy and I were hiking alone on a lesser-known trail that ascended the butte across from the Tetons themselves. As I made the mile-long ascension up the steep terrain of what would be an eight-mile hike, I tuned in to the sound of my breath as I labored up the steep incline. Each step methodical, a meditation and blessing of gratitude of how far I had come since the ski accident. While Jeremy walked ahead of me as he usually did, butterflies flitted around us seemingly everywhere, as if they were beckoning me to continue the journey, their grace and freedom reminding me how I had taken flight myself and as a result was soaring far beyond the life I could have imagined before. Birds of all colors and sizes skipped through the tree line as I continued the climb, and when we both paused to turn back to take in the view of the snowy Tetons peeking through the trees, I finally felt free.

I remembered the moment that a butterfly had rested on a leaf of the apple tree outside my office window in LA a few months after the accident. At that time, I had been so grateful to be able to sit with the aid of a special insert I had purchased from a Relax the Back Store, and while I'd always seen butterflies as symbols of my mom, who had died at the age of 64, the butterfly that showed up this time seemed different. It had sat for a while before finally taking flight in a shock of orange and golden-yellows, and it had hit me then between the eyes. I was now 55, just 9 years younger than my mom had been when she died. If I knew *I had just 9 years to live*, I would not look back at my life as meaningful if I remained stagnant, attached to the 27 years of memories I had created in Los Angeles. And while I had finally achieved everything I thought I had wanted at the time, all my creating had been in service to the illusion that if I were to win at the game of life, then would I feel happy and fulfilled. I had believed a meaningful life was merely to celebrate a series of accomplishments and pepper them with vacations and meaningful moments with people I loved.

When Jeremy and I scrambled the final few steps of the trail hours later to stand on the rocky pedestal and gaze out over the broad Snake River Valley below, I was in awe at the power of creation. The natural beauty surrounding me. The fact that I was there. That I could walk.

"We did this," I said, as we sat side by side, dirty from the trek, on a nearby boulder, splitting the energy bar I had shoved into his backpack earlier that day into two pieces. "We had the idea, then we took action, and we created it."

He leaned over then to kiss me, and I put my hand into his. As a 55-year-old self-professed overachieving control freak with a fear of change, I was not the typical candidate for this kind of courage, but the butterfly I saw that day in my office had carried the whisper of the dream of what was possible, and then the power and beauty of planting seeds had led me to this moment of meaning on the trail with my husband.

And in the process of it all, I had come home to myself.

"I don't miss the life we left behind anymore," I said. "Rather, I feel for the first time I am in creation of the adventure of a lifetime that will forever change me and us and, as a result, the trajectory of my life."

I felt alive.

I had seized an opportunity to change and to create. And in that, all the growing pains were helping me become a more fully expressed, better version of myself. It gave me agency. And power to live a life that felt expansive, a life lived on my terms.

3, 2, 1 . . . Go!

As you study the word *create*, consider what it is that you are going to create. Remember, you experience fulfillment from not just the product you create or the output but also the process itself. When you create, you are in action, and you are in the very being of creation, which is what brings joy, meaning, and fulfillment in life.

Explore where you want to begin exploring and ask yourself some Wisdom-Seeking Questions. (This might be an area of your life that scored low in the Wheel of Life Exercise, but it does not have to be.)

I want you to think about the big ideas and dreams you have had—the things you thought you could do someday. Or the thing you are waiting to do when the time is right. Or perhaps you don't even know what that dream might be yet, and you are searching for clarity on what your next step will be. All you might know is that life doesn't blow your hair back now, though you want it to. Maybe you are stuck in so much fear that dreaming or ideating seems far too terrifying. After all, you might think, why dream when I may end up just being disappointed or let myself down even more?

All perfectly normal.

Perhaps what you want to create is in the area of play or fun, or maybe it's spiritual or emotional growth? Maybe you want to create an insight or breakthrough. Create a new opening. When you consider how this might apply to you more deeply, ruminate on how you might get your hands dirty in a way that puts you outside your comfort zone.

Here are some ideas for what else you can create:

Space—literal or figurative room for something more or time for joy and fun

Experiences that are resonant with your Essential Self

New thoughts or beliefs

New levels of connection or freedom in relationships, thoughts, behaviors, and beliefs

Curiosity. Honesty. Breakthroughs.

Or perhaps you will have an idea for a business or side hustle. Or you want to go back to school to learn a new skill that you thought might only be a hobby. Perhaps you will consider moving to a new location to be closer to family or for a simpler lifestyle. Or you want to spend more time expressing yourself through art. Perhaps you want to move abroad? Now, you might be thinking this is over-whelming, but what I can assure you, though, is that the process of life design we are walking through together in these pages will allow you to take baby steps in exploring all the possibilities.

You are going to tiptoe into it.

Ideation

The Life Design experts at Stanford University describe this part of the design process as "going wide" to push for the greatest possibility of ideas from which you can select. Our goal in ideation is not to simply find a single best solution. Rather, it's to simply take steps toward imagining a range of possibilities that could give rise to becoming potential experiments you could explore as you walk forward in designing your Radical Living Challenge.

This Is a Judgment-Free Zone

While there are a variety of methodologies to ideate, the most common thread in all of them is to defer judgment—that is, separating the generation of ideas from the evaluation of ideas. In doing so, you give your imagination and creativity a voice while placating your rational side. You will examine the merits of each idea much later in the process, so for now the goal is to allow yourself to be in the process rather than attach any part of it to any particular dream you might already have.

RADICAL LIVING CHALLENGE:

Get busy with your own creation.

Step 1: Create Idea Trees

- **Look at the list of words that you listed in the What exercise in Chapter 8.** In the middle of a piece of paper, choose one word that you feel an energetic pull toward from The What and write it down. Draw a circle around it. In the area surrounding that word, draw lines to freely associate five to six new words that link to the word you circled. This is a freestyle activity; do not overthink or judge your words (or your drawing)! Next, add another layer using three to six lines from the words in your tree that link to the word in the center that you have circled. Repeat until you have three layers/levels of word associations. If you get stuck as you create layers on your Idea Tree, connect to your Essence and freely associate whatever words come up in the process.

- Repeat the exercise and begin another Idea Tree, starting by using ONE word that you feel an energetic pull toward from your list of How words or phrases.

- Repeat the exercise and complete a third word tree, starting by choosing ONE word that you feel an energetic pull toward from your list of Why words and phrases.

If you feel like this is hard, trust the process and your inner wisdom. Remember that the process is not perfect and that the journey itself will unlock where you are stuck and what knots or entanglements that might be keeping you stuck. Shush your Alligator. Practice self-compassion. Focus on one of the Seven Questions you have learned so far and identify how practicing a tool you learned in a previous chapter might help you keep moving forward.

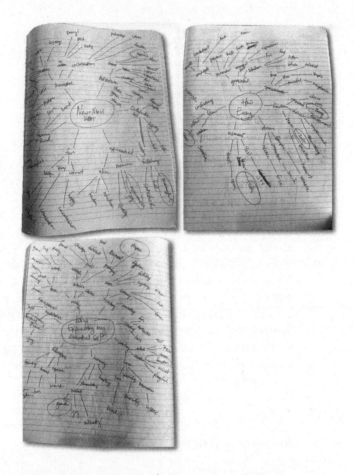

Of course, you can do more than three Idea Trees, and you can do fewer. Finally, if you have other ideation methods you prefer, try one and give it a go! And, if you came into this process with clarity regarding your big dream or idea that can become your Radical Living Challenge, you may want to try this exercise anyway to see what other surprises you can uncover!

Here are pictures of my Idea Tree. The words I chose for the center were:

What: New and Novel

How: Easy

Why: Expression of my Essential Self

Step 2: Marie Kondo that shit!

Next, we are going to declutter your ideas, just like *The Life-Changing Magic of Tidying Up* author Marie Kondo suggests we do in our homes.

Start by circling four or five words that you are drawn to from the outermost layer of each tree that stick out to you. Take a moment with each word and feel into it. Does it resonate? Are you energetically attracted to it? What comes up as you connect to the energy of that word?

For me, the words I chose in my What Idea Tree were: explore, special, experiences, meaningful

The words I chose in my How Idea Tree were: being, soft, faith, slow

And, finally, the words I circled in my Why Idea Tree were: growth, spiritual, purpose, freedom

Step 3: Create Something New for Yourself That Might Not Even Exist Yet

And finally, and this is my favorite part of this exercise, for fun, create fictitious job titles in which your role would incorporate the essence of these words in it. Now, brainstorm something you could create or an action step you could take related to the words you circled or the job title you created. And keep in mind any part of this process might give rise to an idea.

Here were a few of the ideas and fictitious job titles I brainstormed when completing Step 3:

Adventure Meditation Specialist

Director of Spiritual Adventures

I could walk in labyrinths in different countries and write about the experience. I could do my own Eat, Pray, Love *adventure somehow.*

I could visit different countries and write about how food leaves a legacy in different cultures.

I could leave my own nest and write about it.

I could visit female family members across the country and interview them about motherhood. I could design and take classes and create a version of my own master of fine arts (MFA) program.

Remember, at the time I did this exercise, this book or the idea for this book had not yet been born. And as you can guess, the idea to leave my own nest and write about it eventually resulted in the book you hold in your hands. And all that came from scribbling down words.

Step 4: Seek Wisdom through Journaling

Seeking wisdom through reflective journaling—what does the world need to experience that is inside you that you can't risk being lost? In what ways do these words or ideas that you are generating move you toward your definition of success, meaning, and fulfillment that would be uniquely fulfilling for you in a life lived on *your* terms?

Step 5: Get Wild with It

Which of your ideas is . . .

- The most likely to delight

- The rational choice

- The most unexpected

You will carry all this into the next chapters, where we will begin to create your ideal life based on experiments that allow you to explore your ideas in a way that feels exciting and *does not* blow up the life you currently have. (That is, unless you want it to!)

> "Stay out of the future and out of the past.
> Be present to the right now."

Question 5

05 Did You Make Time for Your Spiritual Life?

What this question really asks is: Did you set aside time to listen, to learn and to question so that you can live life in a way that makes you feel like you are in the creation of a life well lived? It asks you to set aside time to pray or listen or meditate to hear the voice of the Divine through the voice of self. Study, then be. Ask, then listen.

Introduction to Question 5

Hopefully now you have a little list of scribbles that might turn into ideas about how you can live life on your terms. A spark has been ignited.

Or perhaps you aren't sure if any of the ideas you have are feasible.

Either way, at this point in the process, some of my clients start to freak out, even if they are excited about the possibilities of what they might create if they were to tiptoe into a life beyond their comfort zone.

Here's why.

They get into analysis paralysis. They are working so hard to create that solution or generate the *best idea,* they default back to:

- Perfectionism
- Overwhelm
- Fear
- Procrastination
- Settling
- Anger and frustration, leading to exhaustion

So, they either give up completely or get so distracted by the searching for the one thing they believe might give them the perfect life that they stop in their tracks.

Don't do that.

Just. Don't.

You are more than halfway through the process and are so close to stepping outside your comfort zone. And there is as much zing in the experience as there is in the result, so shift your focus away from what scares you to the possibility that it could be easier than you could ever imagine.

You didn't come this far to just get this far.

And question 5 is here to help at just the perfect time because it is the one that will help you navigate this part of the journey!

Question 5 asks if you have made time for a spiritual life. However, you can be an atheist, an engineer, or a downright nonbeliever to reap the benefit of question 5. In fact, you do not need to get into yoga, sit cross-legged for hours at a time, be still in a certain place or space, or even be sitting upright in order to listen. You also don't have to quit your job and go live in a yurt on a mountain somewhere far, far away for this to be effective.

And that's because question 5 simply asks if you are consistently making time for stillness—the time and space to listen to your intuition or knowing, to do the work of questioning, listening, and learning because making time for stillness is how you can most efficiently and effectively:

- Identify and feel your feelings so you can manage as well as express them

- Detach thoughts from negative feelings and self-soothe so you can regulate your nervous system as well as lower the cortisol and adrenaline that are messing with your health

- Receive insights and ideas and connect the dots to improve clarity about the challenges you face

- Re-Source energy toward your dreams and ideas through Essence

- Intentionally quiet the mind chatter to create new positive feelings such as gratitude or confidence or self-acceptance

- Think!

Look, I know it's hard to think about blowing up the bridge back to the life you want to leave behind. The Momentum Tunnel of the life you are in now is no joke. And trust me, the Universe will continue to put obstacles in your way that are the leftovers from the timeline that you are trying to extract yourself from. However, once you understand that your Essential Self needs a body and mind to actually make shit happen, you making time for your spiritual life is the opportunity to get direction, the meeting between you and your best self in which you are building and strengthening the channel of communication between you and your wisdom. And that is the most important relationship you will ever have, especially when you are making daily choices to create momentum in the life you want versus the default life you have been living up until now.

CHAPTER 14

Your River, Your Way: Navigating Spirituality on Your Terms

Salmon River, Idaho

When I unzipped the tent that morning a few weeks later, pitched upon the rocky bank of the Salmon River in the largest contiguous wilderness area in the lower 48 states, Andi was tightly tucked into an RV spot near Stanley, Idaho, and the Katz Brothers were at cat camp nearby. All I noticed when I poked my head out was the smell of the air. Maybe it wasn't even the air I smelled, maybe it was the totality of it. The greens and browns everywhere, and the blue sky set against the refrain of the river running and running and the owl screeching in fits and starts, the rhythm offset by chirping birds and the buzzing of wings—I felt like I was inside a moment. Like a leaf unfurling as if it were spring, even though by now it was almost the end of summer.

I looked up and noticed one of the bald eagles, sharp black talons securing her firmly in place, and saw myself through her eyes. A woman in her pajamas and glasses so old they have been put back together with black tape and a look on her face as if she has caught a flower in the exact moment of its full bloom. The thrill in her eyes witnessing this one spectacular, precious moment. In that moment, I think *I am the one that is blossoming on the river.*

When I set my attention back to the task of getting out of the tent and putting my feet into the slightly soggy river shoes I had put outside the tent to dry overnight, I stumbled. And the moment of revelry vanished as I struggled to regain my balance. The truth was, I had also been distracted, teetering on the edge of fear because of what was called the duckie kayak, and I knew that soon one of the river guides was going to ask me again if I wanted to take a turn.

Throughout the trip, many of my fellow adventurers were glee-fully jumping at the opportunity offered each morning and after-noon to sit in the closed cockpit of the duckie using a double-bladed paddle to career solo through the narrow, technical sections of the river. The duckies always followed just behind two large inflatable paddle rafts with a team of six seated along its sides and propelling the raft downstream as they followed the instructions of the guide to navigate the river safely. The largest raft, navigated solely by a river guide and carrying supplies as well as a handful of passengers, usually led the way, and I had spent much of my time on the river on the paddle rafts, in the middle of the pack.

My fear was that if I were to take a turn in the duckie, I would be tossed out into the swirling water, as had happened to many of my comrades. And I was terrified of reinjuring myself. I brushed off the thought, reflexively wiping my hands on my pajama pants, as if the movement itself would restore me to that place of feeling con-nected to my Essence. I thought about my accident and told myself I'm not afraid to do these types of things. It's just that I can't. I'm not able. I swallowed down the fear that arose just imagining myself trying to control and steer the duckie, the river guides and my fel-low explorers looking back at me to make sure I was okay. But then in the same moment, I wondered, is it that I can't or shouldn't, or am I just afraid? Memories of being told I'm an uncoordinated klutz make it all blurry. What is true? What is just what I've been told?

Over the next four days, I became aware of my Alligator taunt-ing me. I hushed it, as I understood this was the Momentum Tun-nel I was trying to leave behind that sometimes grabbed me by the ankles in its effort to keep the old way spinning, telling me I was not capable or that I should be afraid. That I would always be broken. That there was something wrong with me if I said no to the duckie experience.

During my stillness practice on the last morning, I began to understand there was nuance to my thinking that was preventing me from living in the Momentum Tunnel of my now. The wisdom was loud and clear. There is a difference between being afraid to do something new versus *choosing* not to do it. The truth is that on this trip, I had paddled next to the best of them in the six-man raft, navigating through the late-summer rapids in the middle of a torrential downpour, giggling as I was pelted with rain as we paddled. I had also climbed up to the top of a steep and rocky ridge covered in mud in the pouring rain, traversing through rocks and patches of poison ivy to stand under a waterfall descending 25 feet from a creek above. I had woken up in the middle of the night to pee, in a state of sleepy joy, overcome by the stillness in the light of the moon. Above all, I had learned that simply *being* is life-affirming. This was in fact my new definition of success.

After I dressed, I made my way to a spot I had found where I could comfortably pee in the river. On the way back to the tent, I noticed the way two particularly tall pine trees jutted out against the massive canyon walls. It was as if they were welcoming me into the magnificent new day, affirming my bravery to stretch beyond the confines of self-criticism that was embedded in my old identity and the old Momentum Tunnel. Congratulating me. I had chosen, even while on vacation, to create space for a moment of stillness, and as a result, I had overcome the beliefs that had so often put me on the sidelines of life. I felt free.

Let Stillness Be Your Paddle on the River of Your Designed Life

So how was it that I went from scratching out an ideation tree to being able to hear this truth inside me that allowed me to stall the old Momentum Tunnel and build new neural pathways of a new identity? How did I navigate past my terror of breaking bones and possibly reinjuring myself in the paddle raft? How did I experience a lifelong dream I have had to live completely off the grid without electricity or running water? How did I get from my little ideation tree to floating down the middle of what is called The River of No Return, so named because the current is so strong that it can only be a one-way path?

When I completed the homework you have just completed in Chapter 13, I was committed to the exercises and this process as if it were the River of No Return itself. There would be no turning back. As I shared in Chapter 12, the words that ended up on my list included *explore, experiences, meaningful, faith, being, slow, freedom, growth,* and *spiritual.*

At first, I jotted down some thoughts, none of them exactly resembling a fictitious job title or an idea that could solve the problem I had surfaced. But then, a few days later, as I listened to the voice of Essence during my stillness practices, I felt the joy when Jeremy and I spent 10 days exploring the Southwest in a campervan. I felt energetically engaged. In flow. I started to connect the dots and see patterns. I remembered Camp Hitaga. The camping trip I took in my 20s with my ex-husband. I wondered if these were peak experiences in my life and what it would be like to create a lifestyle that aligned with this part of my Essential Self.

Take note, this did not happen because of spending hours looking at the words I had listed on a piece of paper or searching on the Internet, trying to think of ideas. And while none of those are bad, per se, what I want you to understand is that through living a spiritual life in which you cultivate time for stillness, you create spaciousness for the Universe or God or your intuition to co-create *with* you. It's like every time you make time for your spiritual life you embark on the next leg of a giant scavenger hunt, open to the possibility that in that moment, you will get your next clue.

This Is the Moment You MUST Choose Not to Give Up and Stop. Here's How:

You must begin to trust the process, or the old identity and momentum will grab you by the ankles and pull you under. You will default right back into your backup life. Then the question becomes, How do I do this when I have a hard time trusting anything, including myself?

So, to begin trusting the process, your brain needs to understand what, exactly, you are trusting in. I'm helping you do this in two ways. First, I'm explaining my process to you and sharing the process my clients have gone through. Second, as we go together step by step and chapter by chapter through this book, you begin to better understand each of the Seven Questions. Then, as you do the exercises and begin to make small, subtle changes, that reinforces your trust in the process and hopefully yourself.

Then, as you begin to make time for your spiritual life, you get better and better at listening for resonance. You start to follow that sensation as if it were your personal navigation system. You begin to tap into what feels like a "hell yes," slowly moving away from the circumstances and things and people that feel dissonant. And when things get messy, you remember challenges are part of life. You seek stillness and remember they are preparing you for transformation or are transforming you already.

You start to trust yourself and the process and maybe the Universe or Divine even more as you develop and strengthen the relationship you have with yourself, Re-Sourcing internally. You go deeper within. You continue seeking wisdom and start connecting the dots and see patterns, all the while feeling more peace, joy, and calm. You're enlivened because you are busy planting seeds. You're Re-Sourcing internally.

Over time, if you follow the processes laid out here, you too will start trusting the process in a brand-new way, believing that the Universe or God or Divine whatever you want to call it is conspiring *with* you. You start to believe all the silly little affirmations you have picked up over the course of your lifetime.

Affirmations like:

"If not this, something better."

Or

"Life is happening *for* me, not *to* me."

We all have pasts with deep traumas and major losses. A spiritual life enables you to shift how you experience change and challenge. You can start to learn that dissonance, "stuckness," resistance, or even depression and deep sadness is inviting you to look and see what part of you is waiting to be reclaimed or healed. It's a part of you that hasn't been acknowledged before. Or a part of you that has been left behind is looking to come back again. Making time for a spiritual life creates awareness of this and provides you the sweet opportunity to listen, learn, and become more of who you are so that you can experience a life of meaning, fulfillment, joy, and fun!

So, Flow *with* It

It's through the fifth question that you will develop a completely different experience of change. You get to be a creator, creating. You are engaged with life rather than in resistance to it. And it is in this creation that the fire inside you can come alive. You become more trusting and empowered to make changes. You allow the future you imagined inside your old Momentum Tunnel to die, creating spaciousness for your new ideas to seed and grow. You allow something to rise from inside rather than continuing to do it the old way, searching outside yourself for the answers. When you connect within, you will see what you needed is right there inside you. The next thing will come because in this new way of being, you relate to life differently. Courageously. Radically.

RADICAL LIVING CHALLENGE:

Six months after I created that ideation tree, my husband and I embarked on a six-week experiment to test living in an RV full-time as a possible lifestyle that incorporated many of the words from the exercise. Then, while we were on the road heading back to LA from Redwood National Park we stopped in Santa Cruz to have dinner with a friend and her husband. During that meal, they shared their own love of adventure and mentioned rafting as one of the most special experiences they had together.

In that conversation, I felt that familiar ping of resonance.

Six months later, as I sat next to my husband mapping out the itinerary for what would be our full year living in the RV, I remembered that moment in Santa Cruz and conjured the idea of rafting as a possibility while in Idaho. After exchanging a few texts with a friend, Jeremy discovered there were two spots left on a trip that would depart on the exact date we had planned to be in Idaho. We didn't think. We didn't analyze. We both felt the ping and said yes.

And that is how I ended up on the Salmon River, fulfilling this dream. That is how I became free from fear for my physical safety. How I remembered that I am capable. How I freed myself from self-judgment and learned to take on challenges that align with my Essential Self. Each day of the Radical Living Challenge away from what my home in LA had been had become a journey toward the home I had discovered that was inside me.

And it happened because I had prioritized making time for stillness.

This is the time to remember to use this book as a guide. It's a way to continue to course correct. To be patient. When you feel stuck, go back and review the chapters and exercises.

And while you may have words on your Idea Tree, it's perfectly perfect to not yet have formed any ideas or even the fictitious job title. This is the time to trust that the seeds have been planted.

Allow thoughts and awareness to bubble forth and let them sink in. Radical living is not a linear process. Trust the process and give it time to brew.

Step 1: In your journal, reflect on the following questions: How can you define a spiritual life in a way that works within your beliefs? What do you need to revisit or believe to trust the process? What new beliefs about yourself are blossoming that feel like a "hell yes"?

Step 2: Set aside time every day in the next 7 days for 10 minutes of stillness. Before you begin, set the intention to listen to the whisper of your Essence for any insights regarding the words and ideas you created in your ideation tree. Jot down any messages or insights that come up in your journal.

Step 3 (optional): Feeling stuck? Wanna give up? Just wanna co-create with the Divine? Commit to picking one chapter to reread or read for the first time something that you haven't looked at yet, trusting the Universe will guide you to exactly what you need to continue the journey of your own self-discovery.

"To take control of your life you have to learn to get quiet, live courageously, and step boldly into your 'Hell, Yes!'"

CHAPTER 15

Live Like You Are Dying

The Gorge Amphitheatre, near George, Washington

It didn't take too long to drive from Idaho after picking up Andi and the Katz Brothers at cat camp to get to eastern Washington. And it was early morning as my husband and I pulled into the wide-open grass that would be home while attending a three-day music festival. Within hours, this field would be filled with motor homes and travel trailers and fifth wheels, but now it was empty. It reminded me of the empty space I had felt in front of me when I had been trapped in bed, unsure if I would walk again without pain. The nest was empty and so quiet. I had felt lost in all that space.

My thoughts rushed back then to the first experiment one year before and the 36-foot motor home we rented. This music festival had been the first stop on our tour of the Pacific Northwest. As we had watched Tim McGraw take the stage on the first night of the festival, Jeremy and I had made out like teenagers as Tim reminded me to "Live Like You Were Dying." I had rocked back and forth, moving to the music, Jeremy's arms wrapped around me as we stood amid a crowd of mostly 20-something fans wearing cowboy hats and cut-off T-shirts, the sun setting in the distance turning the sky to light pink and then orange. Before the show, we had spent hours at the carnival that had been set up just outside the stage, and my hair had still been wet from having jumped in the giant foam pit like I was 20 again, taking in gulps of giant wet bubbles next to other concert-goers, my feet slipping and sliding over the sticky plastic rubber pit as EDM music throbbed in our ears. I had felt so in love with my husband and my life at that moment. So free.

I had absolutely no idea then that the entire experience since would be not only an adventure in the literal sense but also the beginning of an adventure in what it means to live a meaningful life. That the little list I had made of my What, How, and Why or the scribbled words on my Idea Tree would lead me on a journey that would entail not only exploring places of interest but also my own feelings, thoughts, intuition, responses and reactions, triggers, and behaviors. And through taking *action*, I would create the Radical Living Challenge.

And so, I had wanted this return visit to the festival to be as spectacular as the previous year. I wanted that romance and play-fulness back. As we had pulled into what would be our parking spot for five days, Jeremy reminded me that in just a few hours the tem-peratures were going to hit well over the 100-degree mark. I could see the worry in his face. He was concerned that because we were dry-docking for five days, meaning we would not be plugged into electricity, water, or sewage, that Andi might not be able to sus-tain it. The air-conditioning would have to run on the generator, and even at the maximum level, it could only cool the rig down 20 degrees less than the outside temperature. That meant that it would be over 80 degrees inside. He worried about the Katz Brothers. He worried about the battery. And he worried about how we could ever possibly have fun at an outdoor music festival when the tempera-tures were supposed to break records into the low 100-degree range nearly every day.

He grimaced and went outside to make sure we were parked close enough to a water supply. I stood near the sink and closed my eyes, remembering when I was about 12 years old and feeling the same kind of helplessness as I sat in the kitchen with both of my parents as my dad reeled off a series of sarcastic comments to my mom about her smoking. I had refereed the argument between them, explaining to my mom that my dad didn't really think she was stupid, that he was just frustrated because he loved her. How we all just wanted her to quit smoking. Telling my dad to be nicer to her, explaining how hard it was for her to quit.

This is where it had all started, the need to make everything right. I let the feeling be there for 10 seconds, then 20, and even though it felt like a claw tearing at my open heart, the sensation began to pass. If I were going to live like I were dying, then it was merely my job to live life on my terms, with the Seven Questions as my only guide. It wasn't my responsibility to make this year's festival like it was last year. This was simply me clinging to an attachment of an idealized expectation I held about the past. Reacting to not getting what I wanted in the moment. It wasn't my job to make Jeremy happy either. Radical living wasn't about taking that kind of action. It was about simply being me, now. To take in the preciousness of what is and experience it as unique and important in itself. To delight in the moment in the RV. To embrace the heat and whatever experience it would unfold. To accept it exactly as it was and to take action that enabled me to claim my power and choose life!

I patted Fergus on the head and opened the door of the RV, making my way to the grass, where I saw Jeremy assessing the rig. "Let's blow up that pool you bought!" I said as I walked over to him, taking in the scene of the other motor homes beginning to fill the lot. I could begin to feel the energy of the music simmering inside me.

This was a threshold moment. An opportunity where my stillness practice had allowed me to be present to the part of me that still wanted to make Jeremy happy. To fix situations and change people. But the beauty of the moment also allowed me to find that home inside me I had cultivated. All the seeds I had been planting during my moments of stillness. In that moment, I had remembered to be self-compassionate. To create. To engage with life rather than resist.

There Is No Perfect Time to Take *Action*. So Stop Waiting for It.

The truth is, action precedes clarity.

If you don't make moves, you will never get the feedback on what blows your hair back, or not. And while taking action consistently feels like a big ask, your desires and dreams are worth it.

I have coached thousands of women over the years, and there have been more than a handful who have resisted taking action. They procrastinate, rationalize, or slide back into the waiting game. Some study more. Read another book. Some hide. Some try to make mental adjustments yet never take one step. And some just seem to always have something they deemed more important get in the way.

They have forgotten that doing it perfectly is not the point. And since you can't click a button and wake up in your new life without taking action, the Universe will continue to send messages in lots of different ways that don't feel good, and life just might get harder, feeling emptier and more frustrating than it ever has before.

The Way into *Action* Is to Understand Embodiment

Embodiment is bringing your amazing badass Essential Self to life because transformation can only occur through a lived experience. Think about what it feels like when you are empowered, aligned, and resonant. When you are being *you*. How do you express yourself through the words you use? Think about the way you stand and the way you sit. Embodiment includes how you are expressing your Essential Self yourself through the activities you listed in your What, How, and Why exercise.

Then, think about what it feels like when you are constricted and dissonant.

Without action, there will be awareness, but you cannot think your way into experiencing what you desire or are dreaming of. Without *action* you just stay attached to knots, entanglement, and default behaviors. Without *action* you do not get feedback, and so you will not learn or grow intentionally.

And while you will most likely not embody your Essential Self every moment of your life, when you are in *action*, you are moving forward, even if it means sometimes you take a few steps backward, as I have on the road with Jeremy and the Katz Brothers.

When you and I take action, we are the embodiment of courage, even when we are terrified. And all that *action* is what creates a new identity as a person who lives life on her terms. All this ultimately creates momentum toward the new Momentum Tunnel and the life that blows your hair back.

It's that simple.

And it's your choice. To take action every single moment of every day.

RADICAL LIVING CHALLENGE:

Pull out your What, How, and Why and put it in front of you. You might also want to revisit your ideal day or think about peak experiences in your life. With all that in mind, write three very different stories of what your life could look like in the next five years. You can write in bullet points or in a paragraph. If you want, you can even include images if creativity and being visual is your thing. However you choose to do it, write it as if you are frolicking through your brand-new Momentum Tunnel and everything feels aligned to your Essential Self. You feel inspired. On fire. You wake up knowing you are living a meaningful life simply because you are becoming more of who and what you are.

- One story will be the life plan you already are pursuing, albeit with some new twists as a result of the new foundation you have built here. This is you heading toward that main gate, like we were, hopeful yet flexible.

- One story can be the shocker, the one where you surprise yourself and everyone else in your life! This is the story where time and money are no object. Let the imagination run wild and let people think you're crazy.

- And for the third narrative, consider what might unfold if you were no longer able to continue the path you are on. A big boulder or a closed gate of sorts just blocks you, so what do you do? Remember, this is the opportunity for you to put on paper something perhaps you never dared to speak or even dream of. Write as much or as little as your heart desires. Be specific. Write it from a place of hope. This is your core story.

"A meaningful life is one in which trying and failing feels almost as good as trying and succeeding."

Question 6

06   Were You Hopeful?

This question asks us if we have maintained a life-affirming positive attitude, to focus on the half-full glass, and to be in acceptance of what is while also staying hopeful. It may be one of the most difficult challenges we ever have to face. The question teaches us that we can measure our lives by how well we try.

Introduction to Question 6

How do we truly take measure of our lives? After years of practicing stillness, I have witnessed my Essential Problem showing up in different ways. It's during experimentation and exploration that the parts of you that still need to heal will most likely surface, and when you choose to recognize the power that dissonance is trying to show you, it is not complicated. You can count on being challenged. The beauty is that simplicity and stillness are how you continue to surface the next Essential Problem. And this is your soul's never-ending journey to become more and more *you*.

New Level, New Alligator

What I would discover through the process of experimentation and all I had learned came through to me when I practiced listening. Not in the conventional way, to others, but listening to myself. And what I heard in a moment of radical honesty with myself during stillness was that I had not taken any responsibility for what I had been experiencing with my husband for years. Possibly, ever.

I didn't especially like the message that it was my responsibility when I heard it in that moment. And, what was even more important as I continued to ask Wisdom-Seeking Questions and listen during my stillness practice in the days that followed, what I didn't want to admit was when I had felt trapped by Andi or missed my kids, or when this adventure didn't go as planned in any given moment, I was making my unhappiness *Jeremy's fault*. And the reason I knew this was because I was listening in a new way. And that awareness felt deeply resonant.

When you are still, the invitation is to be free of judgment. To be curious. Honest.

Ultimately, when I surfaced this new problem, I created new experiments, viewing it all as not merely an adventure across the country but an adventure in which I was deepening into becoming more and more my Essential Self. That my soul had chosen it perfectly *for me*.

And in all that, I created spaciousness and freedom because I stopped focusing on what was wrong with my husband. Instead, I became better and better at creating possibilities for myself. To continue learning. To figure out how to navigate the fine line between being supportive and being a fixer. And in all this, I was growing because I stayed curious about how all this might transform my life in a way that would ultimately bring me into an even deeper alignment with myself.

CHAPTER 16

Keeping It Simple

Redfish Lake, Idaho

After spending a week in Washington, Jeremy and I arrived at Redfish Lake Lodge, back in Idaho on our way east. It was mid-August, and the afternoon sun cast long shadows on the Sawtooth Range. Children giggled as they splashed and kicked alongside cousins or friends or siblings in the lake, parents and grandparents with their tanned hands wrapping around beer cozies, looking on from the sandy shore. And I ran to get myself a soft-serve ice cream cone. Everything about this place reminded me of vacation—the wide expanse of beach, the lake. And vacations always reminded me of ice cream.

As I waited my turn in line, the glistening water sent me back to the times I had splashed with my daughters on bright-orange-and-blue rubber rafts decades before, during our trips to Lake Twain Harte in Northern California. We would get ice cream, the girls patiently tucked in between my mom and dad at shaded picnic tables where we played bingo on Tuesdays, waiting for me to come back with their swirls of vanilla and chocolate piled high. Joy had seemed so simple back then.

Minutes later, my own vanilla and chocolate swirl in hand, Jeremy waved me over to come get into the boat he had rented to explore the lake. As we sped across the five-mile-long glacial lake surrounded by the tall peaks of the mountains, the tranquil waters shimmering beneath the falling sun, I reveled in the fact my husband had discovered such a beautiful and somewhat remote location for us to explore. I smiled and felt all of myself relax and fall into the deepest parts of my heart, the memories we had made together like this in the last six months floating in and through me. As we approached the southern shore of the lake, drawing closer to the embrace of the Sawtooth Range that towered around us, the warmth of the sun began to wane, giving way to long, cool shadows.

There in the boat, it became as clear. In every moment, there was an opportunity for me to choose between the light in me and the darkness that was there too. And it was in that instant transition from light and warmth to shade and coolness that I knew why it was so hard for me to feel full, satiated. Satisfied.

It was simple.

Once again, I had created confusion in my mind and stumbled, complicating what I thought was important with what was truly essential. In my life. In me. There had been so many perceptions and beliefs, patterns, attitudes, conditioning, and old behaviors that had been stacked up for decades inside me, and that bundle of history kept interacting with present moments in such a way that confusion and conflict seemed to keep repeating.

It was my reaction to what I was experiencing that was my doing. And to recognize this required humility. I shivered then, feeling the coolness of the mountain shadow envelop me. It was my attachments to the expectations I had for myself and my life that had created a reaction of resentment and disappointment. Never enough. Nothing ever felt like I was living up to what I had expected of myself and others. My responsibility now was to begin to change how I related to all of it. Would I continue to choose the shadow or finally change how I related to what it is that I was experiencing? If I were to truly live life on my terms, then this simple daily choice was my responsibility. Both parts of me there, side by side. It had always been my choice.

There Is No Perfect Way to Do Your Brand of Stillness

When you create time for stillness, there is no perfect way to do it. You do not have to sit cross-legged. Nor do you have to light a candle or sit in front of an altar. What is most important is to find a way of making time for a spiritual life that works for you. Some clients find moments of stillness when they hike or swim or walk. Some find it at church or in a synagogue. My client Andrea loves to sit in a rocking chair in her bedroom in the late afternoons to get quiet. Some clients listen to meditations on apps. Others find meditation teachers. Or go to yoga. I listen to guided meditations each morning after I wake up. And I do it lying down. And while you might fall right back asleep, this works for me. The net result is that you want to experiment with different ways of being still, keeping in mind that the result you are searching for is not to have a moment where you hear the voice of God, forever changed. Or to feel yourself levitating away from your body. The goal is simply to be quiet. Notice your thoughts. Be with your feelings. Practice listening to the voice of your Essential Self. And in my experience, you don't even have to silence your thoughts every single time, even though that is what is often touted as an important skill in meditation. For me, my stillness practice is often the only time I have to think that is free from the busyness of doing.

The only thing I recommend you do is to be consistent. Remember that one of the questions we have discussed asks if you have planted seeds. It is in *creating* time for a spiritual life that you get another twofer. This is how seeds get planted. So do it. Create consistency.

Because we love when we can be efficient here.

RADICAL LIVING CHALLENGE:

Spend 10 minutes in quiet reflection. You can journal using one of the Wisdom-Seeking Questions in the Appendix, use a meditation that you like from an app, or just sit quietly without any distraction and listen. Write down what comes through. What is something you are attached to that you need to let go of to live life on your terms?

"When you get something you don't want, or don't get something you want, face the pain of it now so that you can become more whole."

CHAPTER 17

Embrace the Ongoing Process

Overnight Stop in Garryowen, Montana

By the time Jeremy and I arrived in Garryowen, Montana, I was sick of driving. The slow travel thing Jeremy and I had discussed back in North Carolina had completely been forgotten. We had plans and reservations, and so I had acquiesced. Living in an RV obviously implies one is driving; however, I had not taken into consideration what it would take to get from the rafting trip in Idaho, all the way to eastern Washington for the Watershed Festival, then back to Idaho to check out Redfish Lake in time to get to Glacier National Park in Montana, where we had secured an amazing spot at one of the best campsites in America. Time was of the essence, again. I knew that the extra driving was somewhat my own doing as I was the one hell-bent on going to the music festival, even though it had taken us miles and miles out of the way. And so, I refrained from anything that could be interpreted as complaining.

But the truth was that I was sick of staying overnight in Walmart parking lots. And while I initially was enchanted by the novelty of it, I couldn't stand one more night of the stress of finding a parking spot in what was usually a giant obstacle course littered with parked cars, huge RVs, and fifth wheels. By the time we arrived after seven or eight hours of driving, then doing what was required to put out the sides and set up Andi for the night, only to put down all the shades and hide out under one of the streetlights strategically placed around the parking lot to discourage criminal activity, I was irritable.

This was not what I had imagined it would be like when I set out to travel across America for a year.

I didn't know what to believe in anymore.

I thought of the story a mentor of mine had shared with me that allegedly took place in 1859. A man named Charles Blondin had walked on a tightrope over Niagara Falls, walking 160 feet back and forth between Canada and the United States. Once he crossed on stilts, once on a bicycle, and another time, he carried a stove and even cooked an omelet for the crowds that gathered. Whether the story was true or not I did not know, but the story goes that after walking backward and wearing a blindfold to Canada, he returned, and this time he was pushing a wheelbarrow. He had proven he could do it, and with that he asked the audience if they believed he could carry a person across in the wheelbarrow. "Yes!" they shouted. Of course, they believed he could do it. If he could walk backward wearing a blindfold, surely he could push the wheelbarrow forward with a person inside it. It was then that Blondin asked the question: "Who will get in the wheelbarrow?"

The crowd was silent. Nobody dared to take Blondin up on his invitation.

The story reminded me that hope required more than just words. I can believe, yes. However, believing *in* is something altogether different. It required action, trust. It required faith.

And so, as the sun began to set in the sky, Jeremy pulled out his phone as we approached Montana. I was ecstatic when he suggested we overnight at a quaint nearby campsite in Garryowen.

I needed a place to pause.

A few minutes after we pulled in, Jeremy bounded out of the front office, the campsite map he held in his hand fluttering in the wind.

"Come in here," he shouted, urging me to get out of the rig. "They have ice cream. It's free. And there's a cute little market too."

Thirty minutes later, after putting the two chocolate ice-cream bars in the freezer and setting the homemade potpie we had purchased in the oven, Jeremy decided to use the remaining daylight to wash the massive number of dead bugs off Andi's huge windshield. And I decided to hike up to the top of a nearby peak to catch the sunset.

I plodded up the pathway in my flip-flops, realizing I still didn't believe *in* anything much of the time. I believed selling the house was a good decision. I believed Jeremy wanted the relationship to be better. I believed I was smart and capable of living life on my terms. However, did I believe *in* any of it? I didn't trust. The truth was that I felt terrified.

As I approached the top of the hill, I turned to look out over the wide-open plains, watching the sky turn from pink to orange. I thought of the first time I had practiced having radical faith in the face of something that had felt like walking backward blindfolded over a gorge. When my dad was first diagnosed with a slow-growing cancer, over and over the hope he would survive became obfuscated by metaphorical dead bugs, like the ones that kept slamming into Andi's windshield. No matter how many times I had tried to clear them away, there was always a next thing. Another challenge. And while I knew that he would one day die from cancer, it happened in a way that was completely unexpected. That experience had felt like walking backward blindfolded for months. But I chose to get in the wheelbarrow. To trust. To take a life-affirming positive attitude in ways I could have never imagined and to be present for him during his death in ways that allowed me to experience deep grief while also celebrating his incredible life in the final days we had together. It was in fact that experience that led me to these Seven Questions and to the Radical Living Challenge. Even the book I wanted to write—all of it was a gift from my dad that was changing the trajectory of my life for the better. I knew life was going to happen regardless. And I also knew that having faith and being hopeful was not some nansy-pansy spiritual woo-woo attempt at toxic positivity. I was done with that.

I saw Jeremy below, now balancing on the ladder, his arms reaching up, up, up to the top of the windshield, then back down again, the squeegee in his hand. Repeat. It was clear there was work to do. Like that damn windshield. It would be clear, yes, but then tomorrow there would be more dead bugs.

My thoughts returned to the decision to sell the house. I remembered the moment we drove away for the last time, the moving van not far behind. The belief that I had done the right thing had felt flimsy, like tissue paper. I remembered that belief dissolving into nothingness as I walked into the first house we had rented in Palm Springs, the Katz Brothers in tow. I was disappointed, recognizing within seconds that the pictures of the house online did not reflect what the house we had rented looked like. I had floated through the house, opening doors and closets and cupboards, battling disbelief. I dug my heels into that old Momentum Tunnel upon discovering one of the bathrooms required going outside in order to use it. I had become despondent, the voice of the Alligator raging in my head. "What have you done?" it constantly asked. My torso and limbs melted into regret as I fell onto the floor, surrounded by boxes and the exercise bike and cat litter.

There on the floor, it seemed as if I had merely traded old problems in for new problems, all of them stemming from the same challenges I had been having for years. The truth of it was this was not just a Jeremy thing.

Not at all.

I had stayed loyal to people who worked for me long past their expiration date. My journal was filled with scribbles, notes I had made on what I might say to each one of them if I only had the courage to tell this one or that one their performance was no longer acceptable. Tell them I wanted to let them go. They were always good people, making it hard for me to say good-bye. I believed they had good intentions, but over time, I no longer believed *in* them. Yet I allowed them to stay. I avoided the truth and had put their happiness and well-being before my own needs time and time again. I ignored that dissonance inside me and made promises to myself to handle it next week or next month. But I didn't.

Instead, I complained. Or did the work I was paying them for myself because that was just easier sometimes.

I was letting myself down each time I felt that dissonance and did nothing to make a change until they ultimately quit.

Surviving, yes.

But certainly not thriving and definitely not living life on my terms.

That was how I had operated until I had the courage to get in the wheelbarrow and sell the house in LA.

And take on this challenge.

As the sun began to sink into the Montana horizon, I understood what it meant to have faith. The entire journey thus far was proof the process itself was unfolding in a way that would be exactly what I needed. That I had learned my needs were just as important as the needs of others. That I was capable. That it was not my job to fix and make others happy. These were the exact lessons I had needed to untangle all those knots and "nots" to become more of my Essential Self.

From my perch on the top of the hill, I looked out past the fading sunlight at the RVs below and out into the horizon, and it dawned on me that we were nearly halfway through our yearlong adventure. I was glad this night hadn't been just a parking lot pit-stop. We took a detour and made it work. I tucked the moment into my heart and felt it swell. Joy. Montana. Absolute beauty. I leaned in to faith. Hope. I believed *in*.

And that was a start.

Hope Stems from Faith

The key to changing this approach and becoming hopeful lies inside the principle of radical faith. Faith does not require you to be religious, believe in God, or subscribe to the Law of Attraction. Question 6 does not ask you to fake it until you make it.

In my experience with clients, however, most of them think they are being hopeful but realistically are somewhere in between toxic positivity and good old-fashioned rationalizing. They justify. Intellectualize. Avoid. Their brains, which are pleasure-seeking by nature, are constantly searching for ways to feel safe and comfortable. As a result, they are very good at adjusting their sails to keep the boat afloat in the direction they think will make them happy, or at least feel better. This looks like trying a variety of things they think will solve the problem. The weapons of mass distraction. Things like organizing a closet. Try getting into a relationship. Get out of a relationship. Work harder. Stop watching the news. Get off social media. Get on social media. You get the point. Sinking is rarely an option for these types of people.

This is why of all the questions, "Were you hopeful?" can be the most challenging to answer. Cynics might say that to be hopeful is to set yourself up for disappointment, that being hopeful is foolish. Or, with all the things wrong with the world, there is no hope. When I posted about this on social media, the comments even included the adage, "Make plans and God laughs." I hear you. Living life on your terms isn't about being hopeful in such a way that you are not aware of what is happening around you. Life will happen.

And, because of the negative cognitive bias most of us have in which we mostly see what is wrong in a situation, mastering the principles within this question will be challenging, especially at first. That said, to be in acceptance of what is while still remaining hopeful will also be the biggest game-changer in your ability to live life on your terms.

I can already hear your sigh. But I also know you can do it
To be resilient.
To start.
To fail.
To learn.
To create.
To ask.
To listen.
All in the pursuit of becoming more of who you are.

And it is when you do this that you are truly the creator of your own life. One foot, then the next one. Can you see Charles Blondin on the tightrope? Can you see the blindfold over his eyes? Can you see his hands on the handle of the wheelbarrow? That first foot going backward? Picture him walking over the gorge, hoping to make it to the other side.

RADICAL LIVING CHALLENGE:

Being hopeful comes from a place of acceptance and believing *in.*

When you surrender in faith and hope, you release yourself from the self-created confinement that keeps you stuck in the illusion that the world is painful, unjust, and disappointing. That you are a victim of circumstance.

Rewrite the narrative of your life's journey. Rather than focusing on it from the place of regret or disappointment in your core negative experiences, reflect on how the unfolding of your life thus far has made you exactly ready to begin the process of reinventing your meaningful life.

"If you want to turn the light up in the world, turn it up inside yourself."

CHAPTER 18

LifeCheck Yourself

The Badlands, South Dakota

A week before getting to the Badlands, we had hiked Glacier National Park. There are seven entrances into Glacier National Park. And only three of them connect to the popular Going-to-the-Sun Road—the only road in Glacier that travels over the Continental Divide. It had never occurred to me that a national park could have many entrances. I'm somewhat of a black-and-white thinker. One way in, one way out.

With just a little research, Jeremy and I discovered a hiking trail that would take us to the top of an actual glacier. However, it required us to drive to Many Glacier Entrance, one of the less-popular entrances. It would take a full two hours to get there, but we were excited nevertheless to take a path less traveled. The next morning, when we arrived, the park ranger let us know that the entrance was at capacity and temporarily closed. At this point, it was nearly noon. The hike we wanted to do was five miles out and back, and I did not want to eat the packed lunch I had brought for us in a parking lot. By this time, I was very much averse to parking lots. And so, we bumped our way in the Jeep back down the uneven brown dirt road toward town to get Internet so we could come up with some way to get into the park, rather than wait the estimated two to three hours the ranger had said it might be until the entrance was open again.

Thirty minutes later, feeling defeated, I felt a twinge of intuition and suggested to Jeremy we drive back to the gate. As we approached the entrance this time, I strained my eyes and saw it was completely open! Like teenage dragsters, we cruised through the gate to the parking lot, easily parked the car, and set out to eat lunch on a park bench by the trailhead.

As we began the ascent, we saw a moose, up close and personal. Totally unexpected. And while the top of the trail was closed off because there was still ice and snow, we saw animals drinking from a lake down below and took off on a completely different trail to watch them that led us back down the main trail and back to the car in a way we had not planned on taking.

Things did not go as well in Badlands National Park. Jeremy and I decided to explore one of the many canyon trails, and while it was recommended to hike in the early morning or late afternoon due to the extremely hot weather, it had taken us nearly two hours to drive the Jeep from our campsite to the national park, and it was approaching midday by the time we arrived at the trailhead. The Lakota called the area *mako sica*, or "bad lands" long ago because of the rocky terrain, lack of water, and the extreme temperatures that made it difficult to traverse, and so it made sense the parking lot was nearly empty when we arrived. As we mentally prepared to begin the short out-and-back three-mile walk and changed into hiking shoes, the scorching August sun was already relentless.

The start of the trailhead was clearly marked a few feet away from where we parked, and as we began walking the path that had been clearly marked at the outset, each step sending small puffs of fine, powdery dust into the air, the trail quickly began to turn into a maze of loose gravel and dirt. I looked up, unsure where to go next. The well-worn trail had disappeared completely. I turned my head left and right, and from my place on the trail inside the dusty canyons, I realized I was completely disoriented.

"Does your phone work? Do you know where we are, exactly?" I called out to Jeremy, who was a few feet to the left of me, turning his phone first upside down, then horizontal as he searched for the blinking blue dot that always marked our whereabouts.

"Yes, it's fine," he said, his eyes still on the phone. It was clear he was puzzling out which direction was the way toward our destination and which was the way back to the parking lot. He held out his phone in front of him as if he were holding out a lantern that might light the way. He turned left, then right, trying again to get oriented.

I felt my heart start to quicken as I looked around the canyon, searching for a clear path or other hikers to follow, but we were completely alone. The towering spires of eroded rock rose like ancient sentinels around us, their sharp peaks etching the sky, and the intricate layers of sedimentary rock that lined the dusty trail were various hues of red, orange, and yellow. They all looked the same. Jeremy beckoned me toward him, and in the silence punctuated only by the dry, warm breeze that carried with it the eerie scent of the sunbaked landscape, I took a sip of water from the pouch I was carrying on my back, joining him to assess the situation.

This is the moment where living life on your terms will be difficult. You will wonder whether it was worth the while. This is the time to remember to LifeCheck Yourself. To focus on the Seven Questions and engage in the process of seeking wisdom by asking the right kinds of questions. To create stillness and listen to your Essence. To take on the challenge from a place of hope and radical faith leading you toward the next evolution of your soul. To heed the call and to LifeCheck Yourself as many times as needed as you live a meaningful life on your terms.

Part of me wanted to complete the hike. The other part of me felt choked by the concerns I had that we either were already lost or would become lost and face a night in the canyon unprepared. Would I choose to face the challenge, or was the truly courageous thing for me to do to face the uncertainty of the Badlands and use the data collected from what we had learned thus far and return to the car? To fail fast. I hated not having one clear path. I hated that I could not predict what would happen amid uncertainty.

I wondered, why *this* exact path for my life? I considered the totality of it as I closed my eyes. What were the lessons I had needed to learn? What was it that my soul really wanted that I had been trying to fulfill in a way that was less than ideal? For years, I had muted my own needs to stay on the path so that others might find happiness or so that I could fulfill a goal that was supposed to bring me happiness. I was done forcing square pegs into round holes and falling back into the old and familiar ways so that I could feel in control.

As I stood there, torn between the desire to complete the hike and my overwhelming sense of unease, I realized this moment was about more than just choosing a trail. It was about honoring myself. And my intuition. Tuning in to my truth. I felt the expectations I had put on myself and the pressure to always prove something or to abdicate to someone else dissipate. It was time to trust in what I knew was truth for me. That turning back was not a failure, but an act of courage in itself.

Closing my eyes, I recognized the patterns of self-sacrifice and the habit I had of silencing my own needs for the sake of others' happiness or because I simply didn't trust myself. But in that moment, I made a conscious choice to break free from those constraints. No longer would I force myself down a path that didn't align with my true desires. It was time to listen to the whispers of my soul and to trust that stepping away from the familiar was the next step toward true fulfillment.

Jeremy glanced at me, irritation etched into his features.

I hesitated, but just briefly as I walked toward him. "I want . . . to head back to the car." The words fell from my mouth with new certainty.

His brows furrowed in frustration. He believed I didn't trust him to navigate our way to the end of the trail.

"But we've come this far. Are you sure?"

I nodded, my gaze drifting over the rugged landscape of the Badlands. "Yeah, I just . . . I don't know. Something isn't right. It's hot. I feel done."

Agreement flickered in Jeremy's eyes, and a wave of relief washed over me. "It's time to stop trying to force things."

With a nod, Jeremy leaned in to give me a kiss. The saltiness of it lingered on my lips, and I smiled as he pointed over toward a patch of dust and brush where the blue dot on his phone indicated we needed to go to get back to the Jeep.

Steady Your Foundation

So, as you stand on the threshold of the next badass evolution of you, it's time to begin relying on the solid foundation you have been building internally through the Seven Questions to help you connect to your Essential Self and navigate through the badlands of your own life.

The primary action you will learn is to consistently LifeCheck Yourself. In doing that, will you choose radical honesty and courage, or do you choose to stay comfortable? Will you choose convenience or the entrance to the path that takes you closer to your vision? Will you listen to the voice of your Essential Self or will you "yeah, but" yourself one more time?

When you LifeCheck Yourself, you take that familiar heavy feeling and use it as a signal that there is a lesson ready for you to learn. As you navigate the badlands of designing a life that blows your hair back, you may unconsciously slip back into the position of being a victim of your circumstances, as if you have accidentally wandered into "the badlands." Try to fix the problem you think you have. In order to take on the rocky terrain and impossible heat of the sun, which is life, you need to take responsibility for the experiences you are having. You need to bring water. Wear a hat. And make sure you have a clear path in and a clear path out because the trails are not well marked. And that path is the Seven Questions framework we are working from in this book.

When your What, How, and Why are not energetically resonant to Essence, your energy is depleted. Even though you believe that the need for money or security or comfort will be enough to make something "worth it," unless you find a way to align it to your What, How, and Why, you are working against the flow of the Universe. You are creating more knots and entanglements. Moreover, these experiences usually don't yield the result we are seeking. No matter how hard you try or work on it, focusing on finding the silver lining or some other way of justifying it as a good plan of action, the energy of the Universe always wins.

The truth is that the opposite is true. When you are energetically aligned to Essence, you really start to manifest and experience the kind of material success you are seeking, along with more joy, freedom, and impact.

And more importantly, you must recognize this crucial fact:

Your need to be aligned with your Essential Self is *as important* as any other need you have. Not more important. Not less important.

As important.

I consistently hear clients say they are scared as they make that walk blindfolded into the next chapter of their life. They fear they can't do it or that it will be too hard.

And my guess is that as much as you are becoming invested in some of the ideas you have generated as a result of your experiments, the thought of letting go and walking blindfolded where there is no well-worn path feels terrifying. Even if intellectually you understand where the old limiting beliefs and patterns come from, to create new momentum and a new identity requires that you choose to follow your light rather than return to the shadow of the old Momentum Tunnel, where the Alligators become your house pets.

To stay on the right path toward a life of meaning, you must understand with all your heart that as you live life, you will get thrown off course. This happens when:

- You get things you don't want.

- You do not get things you want.

And each and every time this happens, there is the potential for internal disturbance. You will get triggered. Pissed. From getting stuck in traffic to being passed over for a promotion, that feeling will appear as a rise in your chest, a heaviness in your shoulders, or that knot in your stomach. The external circumstances will always be there, trying to throw you out of the path. You may even have self-doubt and question the decision to take the road less traveled and live life on your terms.

RADICAL LIVING CHALLENGE:

Which of the Seven Questions can you use to LifeCheck Yourself regularly to stay on track and fulfill your vision of a meaningful life? Which question is the door that opens to your right path?

CHAPTER 19

Putting It All Together without Blowing Your Life Up

Glacier National Park, Montana

The next day, after being lost in the Badlands, my mind went back to Glacier National Park just a week before and why the journey unfolded the way it did. Epiphanies often happen in flashbacks, especially when we use Wisdom-Seeking Questions. This is wisdom in its purest form. Everything building to teach me exactly what I needed to know.

This day at Glacier had unfolded so differently from the day in the Badlands because living life on your terms does not mean you stand helplessly in the middle of a desolate canyon with no clear path and go scorched earth on your life. When you are following the Life Design Process and use the Seven Questions, you will clearly identify entrance points you can take to explore living the kind of life you want to live. But one thing is certain: whatever path you choose, the small changes you make in the form of creation and taking action allow you to tiptoe toward a life you love, on your terms.

That day in Glacier, together we had chosen to explore the path less taken, and it felt exhilarating. Of course, like life on the road, throughout the day, there were fits and starts. Unexpected highs and lows. The Universe kept serving it up, and we experienced it all, adapting, adjusting, and finding joy as much as we could, even when confronted with swarms of mosquitoes as we walked the last two miles through a wooded forest just as the sun began to set, having to race against time to get out of the park before the road closed for the night.

The Question Becomes "How Do We Get from Here to There?"

You too are designing your life to simply create more of what you love and to close the gaps in the areas where you feel dissonant. You want more impact or financial abundance. You want freedom. Ease. Less work. Different work. No work. You want to get the things done that are on the list of tasks you have. You want to wake up feeling gratitude and blessed to have a day ahead.

And the only way I have found to navigate through this is by homing in on all the aforementioned practices and questions on a daily basis. Explore all the entrances. The one less traveled and the one that feels like just an expanded or adjusted version of the life you currently have.

You can't go wrong because, as you can see, whatever possible life you choose, wherever you go, there *you* will be. So, the way we stay hopeful and believe *in* the future timeline while we are exploring and experimenting with all the possibilities requires that we double down on living life using the Seven Questions as a foundation.

Do You See How Powerful Having that Foundation while Imagining Future Possibilities Can Be?

The life you have lived until this moment has been exactly what your Essence needed to get to this moment. The moment of taking empowered action and having increased awareness. Yay, you! Your soul has been in service to your new timeline and identity even though you didn't know it. When Jeremy and I instead ventured into the part of Glacier National Park that most people do not take the time to explore, the Many Glacier Entrance, I didn't know that day would remind me that not only are all parts of the journey valuable but also even when your exploration does not go as planned, that pathway is still guiding you toward your next step in the journey.

Experimentation and Exploration Are the Strategies You Will Use Next to Get into Action toward Your Ideal Life

The next step in the process is one in which you start to weave how you feel, think, and act into specific strategies. We call these strategies Experiments—yes, with a capital E. We do this because as humans we are bad at predicting what will make us happy. In order to compensate for this innate flaw, experimenting enables you to take small steps and learn about what you *think* might blow your hair back before you go all in. As a result, you get to look at the Ideal Life Plans you created in Chapter 15, think big, act small, and fail fast. (This means you simply adjust course when something feels dissonant or isn't working in the way you expected. Either way, you are following a path, knowing that things will rarely go exactly the way you expect them to!)

You may experiment with ways to improve the areas of life you noted as ranking lower in the Wheel of Life Exercise you did in earlier chapters or further explore elements of the possible Ideal Life Plans you created in Chapter 15. Either way, the goal of the Experiment is to begin testing your dreams and desires so you can continue to refine what it means to live a meaningful life on your terms. Whatever you choose, as you experiment, you will get feedback on what blows your hair back and what doesn't. This tiptoeing between Experiments will then feel like you are living life rather than letting life live you! You are in the act of creation itself, and when you are outfitted with the Seven Questions as your guides, the process will deliver insights and wisdom along the way. And when some of the Experiments do not go as planned, you will make adjustments, allowing for plans to change as life unfolds.

When you explore and experiment, you:

- Tiptoe into your ideal life without completely blowing up the life you have.

- Engage in the iterative nature of creation, intentionally living a life of meaning that blows your hair back, on your terms. Everything that happens is feedback, and you get to enjoy the process of living life rather than letting life live you, waiting for "someday."

- Receive a new opportunity to understand yourself better. You can fine-tune your What, How, and Why and what resonates with your Essential Self.

- Focus on asking Wisdom-Seeking Questions. *When experimenting, you don't reduce your experiences to "Do I like it or not?"* Instead, continue to ask why and focus on what you can learn about yourself, the problem, and potential solutions to closing the gap between your life now and a life in which your Essential Self is most expressed.

- Never fail. Experiments inform, and sometimes this means going back to the drawing board. However, because life design and, heck, life itself, is iterative, all Experiments can lead to more experimenting. Remember, whether you win or lose, you grow. It's the golden rule of Radical Living!

- Get more practice experiencing resonance and dissonance as you explore. And sometimes, Experiments reveal that not only did you not get the solution right but also that the problem you thought you had wasn't exactly the problem.

What is an Experiment that allows you to tiptoe into life on your terms without going scorched earth on the life you have?

An Experiment is a way to try out a new concept or way of doing things, to make a discovery or to test a hypothesis. Here are some ideas for Experiments you could design:

- **Conversations.** Take one of your ideas to start qualitative research. This means speaking to people who are already doing something (or a component of something) that you are interested in exploring. For example, if you are interested in leaving the corporate world to become a solopreneur, you may have conversations with others who have made the leap.

- **Observing.** Observe something similar to what you might want to do yourself. In this kind of Experiment, rather than participate in an activity or speak to someone who has done it before, you observe to understand what it's really like to do that thing. For example, if you dream of opening a coffee shop, observing would look like you spending several hours at your favorite and least-favorite spots. Notice the details while you are there. If you are interested in traveling abroad, join a group on social media just for expats and observe what questions people are asking. Read answers, gather information. If you want to write a book, listen to other writers and see if it feels like you have found something you want to explore and experiment with further, or not.

- **Test and scale.** Shrink the big dream to something that might be like trying it out. For example, instead of deciding to open that coffee shop, you could briefly work at a cafe to understand what it is like. In this case, you would also be having conversations with the owner and other employees. The customers. And you could observe as well as participate in this kind of experience directly. Want to be a writer? Take a class and draft an essay. Try to sell it to a magazine or publish in a literary journal before going for a whole book or screenplay. Dream of living in Europe? Arrange an Experiment in which you live abroad for 30 days.

Make sure your Experiments include real-life experiences so you can embody the process fully!

Create your Experiments in a way that feels like an experience you can react to rather than simply evaluating an idea using logic only. Don't just read about an idea. You must get into *action,* remember? Bring multiple Experiments to the field to test as a basis for comparison. Comparisons often reveal latent needs you didn't even know existed!

First, get clear on your limiting beliefs as well as your goals going into the Experiment.

As I mentioned in a previous chapter, when Jeremy and I did our very first Experiment, we rented a small campervan for two weeks. The questions we had were varied, from if it was possible for us to live in a small space together for an extended period of time to if the trade-off of being able to camp in remote spaces as a result of having a small vehicle was worth living in more cramped quarters.

After we experimented with the campervan, we decided to test a bigger vehicle to see if we could live in it full time. The Experiments we were testing in the 36-foot RV included one of my limiting beliefs, which was that I would not be able to maintain my exercise routine. I also wasn't sure I could work effectively on the road. I had to consider why I believed that to be true. I created specific goals, such as being able to strength train four times a week and cook healthy meals more often than not. I also had to get the technical specifications of what I needed as far as reliable Internet. And as a result, for the six-week Experiment, we purchased an inexpensive exercise bike as well as an easy-to-fold weight bench. We brought a punching bag and dumbbells and kept it all stored inside the RV to use three to four times a week. We also tested different types of Internet solutions so I could work without interruption. We even tested what kind of cooking supplies were essential based on what we had learned after living in the campervan for two weeks.

Here are some examples of questions your Experiment can answer:

- What does it look and feel like day-to-day? Does that align with what is important to you? Does it resonate?

- Let me try a version of this idea. Will I actually enjoy it?

- Does it provide me with enough _____?

- X is really important to me. Will I be able to get that if I do Y?

- For experiments related to your career, you can ask, are there other people making money doing this? Is there a way I could make money doing this?

How to Create Your Experiment

I want you to consider what would you do if you lived like you were dying, as the song goes.

Step 1: What are two or three ideas from your Ideal Life Plans in Chapter 15, the life lived on your terms that you want to explore further?

Step 2: What questions do you have about each of those ideas?

Step 3: Brainstorm three to five ways (or more) that you could answer each of these questions through an experiment (conversations, observations, or test and scale). Remember, you are brainstorming only. You are not required to do any of them. You get to decide later!

Step 4: What Experiments will you do within the next two weeks, and which will you do within the next few months? When do you want to carry out your first Experiment? What is the expected amount of time this Experiment will take? Map out when you will do it.

Step 5: What kind of resources might you need to implement the Experiment? What kind of support or help will you need?

Step 6: What are three to five specific steps you can take right now to begin executing an Experiment?

"Trust your decision to live life on your terms and allow the souls of others to have their journey too."

Question 7

07   Did You Recognize the Blessing?

Have we all taken full advantage of what we have? Do we live with childlike wonder? Have we appreciated the gorgeous sunset or felt the sand in our toes? Were we grateful? Did we see the beauty in the chaos? We are asked, did you live life in a way in which all time is precious and valuable? Did you learn, teach, create, and wonder, and did you help others see the beauty so that they too could be fulfilled by, in the words of poet Mary Oliver, their "one wild and precious life?"

Introduction to Question 7

You are now ready to dig into the last of the Seven Questions.

And look, I know you probably understand the power that gratitude can have in your life. But in question 7, we are asked to dig deeper because recognizing the blessings is simply not just about an accounting of the good shit in your life.

You will often forget about wonder when the day-to-day grind feels like a slog. Maybe you become a thrill-seeker instead, looking for the next hit of dopamine to wake you up. Addicted to drama. And in between those moments, you take on numbing and avoidant behaviors.

In short, the blessings get blurred until you hear about a tragedy or are faced with a loss. Then you seem to count those blessings. This exercise beckons you to craft a life brimming with the radiance of everyday experiences, where light and delight and wonder can be found in the most ordinary of moments. These moments are not just precious in themselves; they are the very threads that weave the fabric of your existence, transforming the mundane into the magnificent and turning every experience into a blessing.

CHAPTER 20

Living with Childlike Wonder

Cedar Rapids, Iowa

Jeremy and I next drove to my hometown of Cedar Rapids, Iowa, to attend my cousin's wedding. It was the end of August. Sitting in the passenger seat, I waited for the scenery to shift from endless fields of green and mostly dilapidated farmhouses to midsized modern office buildings and car dealerships, my eyes flitting from one corn-field to the next as we headed onto Interstate 380. Then, as Andi rounded the final turn before the exit that would lead us to the campground, my eyes drifted, as if guided by a force of their own, to where there had once been a bustling casket factory, established in 1854, but had ultimately been transformed into something far more personal—the birthplace of my great-grandfather's legacy. That building had been a landmark in the small midwestern town where I grew up and the home to the business my ancestors had built in 1915.

I remembered the elevator in the building, the relic of a bygone era, and the trepidation I felt as a seven-year-old approaching the elevator's cage. It was made of sturdy iron that bore the marks of a hundred years of use. I could still feel my dad's smooth hand in mine as we would walk together through the metal gates, worn and weathered. How they clanged and rattled as they opened and closed, the walls adorned with layers of chipped paint, and the wooden floor, worn smooth from decades of foot traffic, creaked underfoot. The smell of untreated hides and fur, slightly musky and primal, still lingered in the background of my senses. The wool, with its warm and comforting scent and the subtle hint of the tanning agents and natural oils used to preserve the hides and furs, added a layer of cozy familiarity to the mix. And while the building itself had been demolished in 1997, whenever I had visited that place where my dad and uncles and cousins had worked for decades, it had been an anchor to me, a connection to my roots. To the beginnings of what felt like home.

I pointed out to Jeremy the hospital where I was born just as it appeared and then vanished again as we quickly exited the now-busy freeway. I recalled a moment in the sunlit closet in my home in Los Angeles. When we were packing, I had been so careful in stowing away the yellow-and-white blanket my grandmother had lovingly hand-knit, the one that had swaddled me on the day I was born. The Polaroid of the moment in front of the hospital doors is forever captured. Me in the blanket being held by my mom. Her beehive, perfect. The dome-like shape teased and styled, framing her 22-year-old face. My father, standing tall in front of the car, was ready to take me home.

As Andi continued to push her way through the streets of my childhood town, I saw the YMCA, the place where my brother had played basketball with my dad, a sacred space into which I was not invited. Yet I could still vividly imagine the stench of the place as we drove past. I could hear the squeaking of the shoes against the decrepit gym floor, their laughter echoing in my ears, a chorus of the shared moments I had longed to be part of.

And the tree-lined street I had lived on that had once been so pristine with its manicured lawns had now faded with age. There were cracks in the pavement tinged with bits of moss and small weeds. The house where I had lived in until I was seven, that my parents had built from the foundation, seemed to sag and was in desperate need of a paint job. The sidewalks where I had first learned to ride a bike were cracked now too, jagged, and thin like lightning bolts frozen in time. I remembered my dad's reassuring hand gripping the back of the pink-and-white banana seat as he guided me. Both of us wobbly. Uncertain.

With each mile we drove, I felt the weight of time pressing on my heart. The years had rushed by, sweeping me along until the accident had forced me to stop. I had let so many precious moments slip through my fingers.

Then it hit me.

This is where the shame of being me had taken root. This is where I had learned to put my needs on the back burner. To please others. And as a result, I had been hurtling through time, swept up in the old Momentum Tunnel, tripped up and entangled in all those knots ever since.

I had spent so much of my damn life preoccupied about what was *not* working. All I had seen were the cracks in everything. Things to work on. To fix. I had been remiss at experiencing the blessings of it all, the blessing that it is to be alive. To be. To take a breath and see the light and possibility. To wake up each day. To feel the blessing of the paths my ancestors had walked so that I would not have to.

I had broken my back, and it had set me free.

This journey. This Radical Living Challenge. It had taken me home. Truly home. To the Essence of me. To the childlike wonder I had in the Polaroid. That day in the yellow-and-white blanket. That day in 1966.

RADICAL LIVING CHALLENGE:

Build the muscle of wonder by trying out this three-step daily practice for six days.

But what is the difference between gratitude, appreciation, and wonder, exactly?

Gratitude is a static intellectual experience. You may say you "feel" grateful, but you probably don't truly feel it. It's just a statement.

Appreciation is a felt sense of that experience of gratitude in your body. It's deeper.

But wonder has a sense of awe to it.

Now, keep in mind that it takes quite a bit of courage to allow this much appreciation in because the moment you feel all that joy, the Alligator often gets activated and turns up the volume between your ears, reminding you of your vulnerability. That things change. That your heart might just get broken as a result of all that love and appreciation. To feel the joy of your blessings, you are brave enough to not only risk it all but also to know that even amid chaos and change, you are still and always blessed.

Step 1: Write down an intention today that incorporates one of the Seven Questions. Examples:

- I intend to breathe deeply, through my nostrils, at work today.

- I intend to connect more fully with my children today.

- I intend to be open today.

- I intend to trust more.

Step 2: Write down three things you are looking forward to today that you want to approach from a state of wonder.

Step 3: At the end of the day, note in writing three things that caused you to experience delight and wonder. They may or may not be related to your intention or the things you were looking forward to.

At the end of the six days, reflect on this question in your journal: What is possible for me if I recognize that all moments are precious and valuable?

"Try wonder as a worldview. Stay curious."

CHAPTER 21

Becoming the Hero
of Your Story

Acadia National Park, Maine

"WARNING: This trail follows a nearly vertical route with exposed cliffs that require climbing on iron rungs. Falls on this mountain have resulted in serious injury and death. Small children and people with fear of heights should not use this trail."

As I approached the dirt path that would lead me up Champlain Mountain, the sixth-tallest peak in Acadia National Park, a few weeks later, I felt the familiar pang of fear as I read the warning sign at the start of the trail.

"You will be fine," Jeremy said, pointing toward the line of cars parked nearby. "Look. Lots of people are doing this hike. You *can* do it."

I pulled my baseball cap down tighter on my head to block the shards of sunlight peeking through the clouds and began the ascent. It started with going over the easy-to-navigate formal granite staircase. I climbed over the first outcropping of boulders using the two awkwardly placed iron rungs, Jeremy boosting me up and over the rocks. A surge of strength pulsed through all parts of me. I could do this.

I thought about all the first steps I had taken thus far in this quest for a meaningful life. I exhaled. One step at a time. Like Charles Blondin walking his tightrope. There had to be the first step. Then another. Except this time the blindfold was gone, and I could see.

I looked at the trail ahead and reflected on the long distances I had hiked in the last eight months, breaking personal records in elevation and miles. The path I had climbed to the Chandelier Waterfall during the rafting trip with switchbacks that zigzagged up a steep hillside. The choice I had made not to navigate the river on my own in a kayak. The miles I had ridden my bike in Hilton Head, the salty sea breeze, my hair dancing in the wind, streaming back like a banner of liberation.

I felt enlivened now in a way I had never felt before, as if God or Universe or Spirit were the animating energetic force within, bringing me strength and courage in a new way. I now understood that fear was not a limitation but a window through which I could see and make choices. I knew that I could assess and adjust along the way.

One careful step at a time I climbed, making sure to maintain three points of contact with the mountain at all times, bantering with other hikers. I paused then. The next section of iron rungs and ladders would take me straight up a flat square piece of granite with a steep drop just to the right. I wiped my hands on the legs of my khaki hiking pants and began my ascent up the sheer rock face. Just me and the towering cliff, eye to eye, reminding me of all the internal walls I had constructed within myself in an effort to fight change.

And to think in doing so I had almost missed out on the living.

My breath quickened, and the sound of the wind whistled past as I continued sure-footed, capable. With each step, I extended my arms upward, reaching for the next sturdy metal rung above me, placing each foot on the ladder carefully, holding on tightly as I climbed. I felt weightless, free, like the falcon that made his home on this trail. So present that the thrill of the feat I was tackling became merely a low thrum. I had always had the power to create my life. One small step at a time.

I had just forgotten.

Reaching for the final rung, the moss-covered rocks framing my path, I felt the grit of the ladder on my fingertips and glimpsed the faint traces of graffiti left by adventurers who had come before me. There was no adrenaline or heart-pumping fear. I grabbed the next perfectly placed iron rung and looked out over the forest and below to the water, dangling there for just a moment, taking in the incredible view.

I had become the hero of my own story.

Sunlight fought its way through the dense blanket of clouds. Jeremy was just behind me, and carefully I pressed my foot against the narrow metal step, hoisting myself upward, using the ladder's structure to leverage my body to the next ledge. The leaves, once vibrant, tumbled gently around me as I stood and readied myself for the next set of ladders just ahead.

There would always be this ebb and flow of beginnings and endings, creation and destruction, birth and death. Dark and light. It was hard to comprehend how a ski injury had begun a transformation that had seemed as insurmountable to me as this hike could have been if I had listened to my fear.

I had risen to the call of adventure deep within my soul and had listened to my Essence throughout. I had overcome obstacles and crossed thresholds along the way. Each and every step, like the rungs of the ladder I now found myself on, had been anchoring me to a new identity that felt more resonant to who I had become. And as a result, the cumulative impact of the decisions I had made along the way had taught me the answers I'd been seeking when I felt challenged were mostly within me. Each step represented an action I had taken to create new momentum toward the life I was creating where I was living life, rather than letting life live me.

I felt alive. I felt whole. But I knew, deep within, that my journey was far from over. As I looked ahead at the next set of rungs and yet another cliff to ascend, suspended between earth and sky, I grasped a truth so profound, the mountain itself seemed to whisper the words to me: I was not just an adventurer; I was the very creator of my own destiny. Beyond this ascent, a final descent awaited—anointing my steadfast vow to welcome fear, forever dedicated to living life on my terms.

Faith Requires Action

Having now read most of the pages of this book and completed the exercises, you too are now teetering on the precipice between the known and the unknown, on the threshold of action, of doing, and not merely dreaming. The lessons from the Radical Living Challenge had urged me to seize life with both hands and become the architect of my own destiny. As you have learned by now, Radical Living requires that you too have faith and that you listen for that resonance inside you, even when the challenges and obstacles along the way may feel insurmountable.

That you take action and do the damn thing.

Of course, along the way, there will be mountains. Some you will choose to climb, and others you will circumvent to find another way. But above all, you will be in the creation of your meaningful life, trusting life is fluid and that using the Seven Questions as touchstones to guide you to that place of internal stability along the way will help you evolve, redirecting and course correcting you when necessary.

Your responsibility now is to be authentic, to be you, and to source the energy of that Essence consistently internally through your stillness practice. To trust the Universe is conspiring *for* you. *This* is how you ensure you are living life rather than letting life live you.

This is your Radical Living Challenge.

So Now What?

I love this question.

It invites you into the all-important moment of self-responsibility. It invites you to create and take action. To not only design experiments but to fundamentally know that all of life is an experiment. To create and engage in life from the lens of experimentation, assessing and adjusting along the way as you intentionally propel yourself toward a meaningful life aligned with your Essential Self, your soul.

The Iteration Phase: Understanding the Assess and Adjust Model

Iteration is fundamental to good design. And so, in your journey of Radical Living, you intentionally iterate by cycling through the Life Design Process again and again and by iterating within a step. For example, by creating multiple Experiments or trying new ways to ideate and continuing to surface Essential Problems. Generally, as you take multiple cycles through the Life Design Process, your focus will narrow as you learn, and you will find yourself moving from working on a broad concept to the nuanced details of implementation.

Jeremy and I started with broad Experiments. We wanted to test different places to live. Then we narrowed it to experimenting with a lifestyle. Again, we narrowed and chose to Experiment living in a small RV. We refined it further, testing things out even more in order to choose the right vehicle with the right features. And along the journey we had continued to assess and adjust, asking questions and making notes on the places we visited and experiences we had, gathering data about what truly blew our hair back.

With Experimenting, There Is No Such Thing as Failure

As I have said, Experimenting invites you to think big, act small, and fail fast. This process will give you clarity as you walk the path of life design as to what your ideal life can look like. And if you remember what we discussed in Question 2—that each and every attempt you make at rising up from setbacks is to repair and heal what is within you so that you can continue to ignite the spark of your Essence—there are truly no such things as mistakes. In fact, the Experiment and Explore phase of Life Design makes thinking big, acting small, and failing fast somewhat of a delight. And as you know from question 1, it is the cumulative impact of your actions that provides the wisdom to move forward. Experimenting is a way in which you no longer must wait to create a life you love. Each small Experiment is an act of creation that results in a feeling of living life to the max now. And failures are there to continue directing you in a way that connects you more deeply to your Essence.

If you remember the first aha I had in which I wondered how the peak experiences in my life could become my day-to-day life, living in Andi full time was just one part of that overall journey. And while the process of life design I have taught you is shown in a linear progression to make it work within the pages of a book, understand that as you live your Experiments and iterate, you will simply rely on the Seven Questions to cycle through getting clearer on your Essential Self and what blows your hair back, both of which will undoubtedly lead to discovering new Essential Problems to solve along the way. New ideas and opportunities will come into your life. More awareness. And once you begin to listen, your Essence will continue to inform you through resonance and dissonance about what you want, what you need, and what you will explore. And in all that, you will weave in your feelings and thoughts with actions and strategies that are flexible, continuing to refine and evolve as you go.

My intention is that through it all, you will experience joy, peace, and the meaning and fulfillment that comes from experimenting and truly living an aligned and resonant life. And that all of it creates new momentum. That you will find yourself, as I have, in a new and exciting Momentum Tunnel that has been activated and animated via your new more aligned identity, an identity that will continue to emerge as you iterate, explore and experiment.

How to Assess and Adjust After Your Experiments

When you complete an Experiment, it's important to review your results and your testing questions. It is in strengthening your awareness and understanding your Essence and what blows your hair back that you can continue to test and refine.

Here's what that process looked like for us, taken from my actual journal:

- I like the feeling of being in a small town in which I can walk easily to things that I use regularly. For example, from a bookstore to a coffee shop to a gym, I want it all to be easily accessible. The town can't be too small, as I learned I do need access to a big-box store and a hair salon and a great health food store. Moreover, that I can access those things within a 15- to 20-mile driving distance. For example, certain towns we stopped in were small and surrounded by nature; however, there was only one main street in town. Or it was too rural to provide us with a good green juice or vegan cookies.

- I love being in a community with active people. What blows my hair back is to be in a community of folks who are eating and living healthfully and are involved in outdoor activities. Jeremy loves water and surfing. I'm learning that while I love the ocean and beach, I prefer mountains, lakes, and rivers. We both realized we are open to exploring how we could find a lifestyle that includes both of those things down the road. We also like being in a community of other people who share other common values like travel and adventure, family, and living consciously.

- We desire a community of people who are also in a time of life where they are creating and enjoying the freedoms of financial security and stability. Our Experiments taught us that while we loved being in and around communities of retired people, we are not ready to make that kind of place our home. On the river-rafting experience in Idaho, we met other middle-aged men and women who are working and live mostly healthy lifestyles while investing in their personal growth and development. It made us aware that there are communities of these kinds of people that we felt a kinship toward and that we wanted to further explore those kinds of communities along the journey.

- I desire more simplicity in my life, not just in the way of living with less things per se. But it's important that I have fewer moving pieces and parts to my life. I don't need to overcomplicate things, from making decisions to how I operate my business and what I need from my partner. In addition, I learned the kind of business I thought I wanted to build was becoming more dissonant to me. I was beginning to wonder if the vision I once had for it was mine or had been born of a "should." I was becoming less energetically engaged in having business obligations on my calendar that felt restrictive of my freedom. Managing a big team was becoming less interesting to me too, as I also became less excited about the kind of coaching I had been doing before. I noticed my energetic engagement and flow became very high when I was coaching the clients who worked with me beyond the scope of relationships. The more I worked on this book and applied the principles in my own life and in the lives of my clients, we created great results. It was both meaningful and fulfilling.
- Andi wasn't necessarily giving us the freedom we had once thought we would have living in an RV full time. We were feeling constricted by timelines and miles. And her size. And the complication of finding a cat sitter for the Katz Brothers if we wanted to travel by plane together.

To continue your own exploring through experimentation, assess by asking yourself the following questions:

- Did you feel energized or drained? Resonant or dissonant? Did it feel like it was in flow or forced?

- Were you energetically engaged or bored? Did you actually like this? Or do you feel like you should have liked it?

Then, Look at the Bigger Picture. Take the Bird's-Eye View.

Overall, what worked and what didn't work? What are the common patterns or themes? What do you want to take forward, and what do you want to shift or change as a result? From this vantage point, you can go back into the Life Design Process and create a new Experiment or make a decision that is resonant with an aligned life lived on your terms. It is this exploration that allows you to transform your life without blowing up the life you have worked hard to achieve. As we discussed in the study of question 1, the cumulative impact of all your decisions will provide you with the wisdom you need to continue advancing forward in creating a meaningful and fulfilling life you love.

RADICAL LIVING CHALLENGE:

For each one of the Experiments you engage in, ask yourself the following questions: Did I actually like this, or did I feel like I should have liked it? Were there any common patterns or themes to what you enjoyed and didn't enjoy that can provide insight moving forward? Are there any limiting beliefs (LAICS) that arose that you need to work through? Ask yourself, what you get from life when you are the hero of your own story.

"You're the hero of your own story."

CHAPTER 22

If It's Not a "Hell Yes," It's a No

Steamboat Springs, Colorado

The sky wore a soft, muted gray, and it felt as though I had ascended into the heart of a cloud.

The evergreen trees stood tall on either side of me, cloaked in a heavy layer of snow, as if each branch had been dipped in the fluffiest marshmallow I had ever seen. And while I knew the rugged Rocky Mountains were there stretched out before me, I saw only the nearly empty trail ahead.

Just me in new purple ski bibs.

I inhaled the crisp mountain air, tentative but confident. On this day, fear had no hold on me. My body seemed to remember this.

The dance of skiing an old, familiar tune.

As I turned my skis downhill, I could feel the mountain below the nearly 200 inches of snow between her and me. It was as if she and I were destined to do this thing together—to create this symphony of potential and of promise. I moved with precision as I began the descent, guided by an intuitive knowledge that transcended muscle and bone, of conscious thought. It was as if the accident had never happened, as if the passage of time had healed not only my body but also my ability to believe in.

Finally. Finally. Joy.

Just joy. That is all I felt as I carved my way through the pristine snow, the freedom of the moment, this liberation from fear, the mountain itself my partner and teacher. Reminding me at first, but then the truth rushing in. Whooshing in.

All the parts of me that had been lost. Since the accident.

Before it.

The profound sense of being authentically myself as I welcomed the cool rush of wind against my cheeks, the rhythm of my heart mirroring the rhythm of the life I had chosen to live on my terms.

Oh, this.

This was a celebration and a dance.

My hair blown back even as it was tucked tightly inside my helmet.

My skis, an extension of my body, responded effortlessly as I intentionally transferred my weight from edge to edge. All this reminding me that I had discovered the inner balance to keep navigating.

To lean in to life.

Each turn, a new challenge. And a new sensation.

My journey down the mountain became a blessing. The profound message I had heard and chosen to embrace—a message of change, of transformation. The beauty in riding the ever-shifting terrain of life.

During the descent, the snow and trees became a blur of motion, a rush of sensation. It was never about controlling change; it was about embracing it with grace and courage.

The mountain, like life, was in constant motion, and my ability to lean in to it was a reflection of the resilience I had learned. It was as though I had learned to dance with change itself, each curve and twist a celebration of my capacity to thrive.

The mountains, the snow, the wind—all spoke of the beauty of change and the thrill of a life of meaning. I was not merely a participant.

I was the creator.

I had asked questions in seeking wisdom. I had returned to me.

I had learned honesty. And I had created.

I had discovered wonder. Recognized blessings.

Been still.

And in it all, I had been hopeful.

I remembered the ski run that began the journey more than four years before, filled with appreciation at how it had led me to build a new foundation. How I had learned to ride the bumps and obstacles of life with more grace, confidence, and joy than I ever did before. And while I had believed then that I might never ski down-hill again like that, I knew that whatever I was going to face in the next part of my journey, I would make a choice.

And that the answer of resonance, however small or unsure, would feel like a hell yes, because living life *that way* is what is radical.

And what is radical is courageous.

And to live a courageous life is to live a life of meaning. I knew I had found my "hell yes."

Living a Life You Love on Your Terms Right Now Is Happening

I couldn't be more thrilled that Radical Living and the art of making conscious change in your life is starting to catch on. But chances are, you might be the first of your friends to take on a Radical Living Challenge. And it would make sense that your friends or colleagues or even your family might roll their eyes at you when you try something new. However, welcome to the world of Radical Living. But to those unfamiliar with the system, it might appear to be a crazy or risky approach to life.

And so, as you design those Experiments or tell your best friend you are thinking of chucking it all to go live in Portugal, you might hear the naysayers reminding you of what you have worked so hard to have, warning you that you could lose it all. But that's okay because you are in good company. You are among those who live courageously and have decided to play the game of life full out!

Daily—literally, every single day—I work with people who are living a designed life, and they share how applying the principles you have learned here have turned their lives around.

I rarely forget a name, but I remember the stories. Like the 55-year-old who, after resigning herself to working in banking until retirement, decided to retire early and not only fulfill her mission to create a legacy by joining her elderly father in his business but also have the freedom to sail whenever she wanted to with her partner, whom she met at her sailing club. Or a single mom by choice who decided that the big consulting agency she built was sucking her life dry, leaving her too tired and exhausted to spend time with her daughter or to date. Then, after learning how to live courageously and apply what she learned about Radical Living, she took her business down to the studs and let go of most of her expenses. In the meantime, she started experimenting with starting a coaching business. She let go of some of her mom guilt and started getting babysitters so that she could date. This way of living allowed her to create a stable income as she slowly built her coaching business and meet her partner, with whom she has lived for the last few years. This approach allowed her to increase her income and finally have the family she had always wanted. I've heard from countless CEOs and entrepreneurs who got their confidence back, their joy back, their sanity back, their weekends back. People who are no longer plagued with anxiety, insomnia, and other ailments caused by the challenge of letting life live them.

This is Radical Living.

And to all this I say make your life a giant *"hell yes."*

Create a life that blows your hair back.

RADICAL LIVING CHALLENGE:

After going through this process, what in your life is starting to feel like a hell yes?

"To live a courageous life is to live a life of meaning."

EPILOGUE

Jeremy and I have landed in Colorado, for now. When my 21-year-old daughter Willow came to visit for one week with her boyfriend, Jack, end-of-summer showers gave us the opportunity to sit at the kitchen table, playing games. Specifically, *Bananagrams*. It was a new game to the three of us and it's like *Scrabble* in that players arrange letter tiles into a grid of connected words. As we began to play, we all became very excited about our words. I mean, very, very excited. The rain was falling, and we were inside that kitchen, squealing with delight. We loved our words so much that we all began taking pictures of our words. The conversation looked something like this.

"Oh my God! I just did *soliloquy*."

"Oh snap! I just used my *X*. *Botox*!"

And being that this was the party edition of the game, there were two tiles with scribbles of bombs on them. The rules state that if you pick up these two tiles from the pile when you are picking, you can give them to an opponent, forcing them to completely blow up their entire board.

And so there I was playing the game, very proud of my flipping amazing words!

And then Jack looked over at me as he raised his eyebrows, the biggest grin ever forming on his face.

"I'm bombing you," he said, handing me his two black bomb tiles.

My heart fell.

"No, no," I said half laughing, and half distraught. "These are my words. Look at them!" I cried. I looked at my daughter and at Jack. Everyone was laughing, including me, except I was seriously sad about the impending loss of my beautiful words.

"No, no." I went on. "The game is almost over. I was going to win!"

And guess what I did?

I grabbed my phone and took pictures of my favorites, to save them and show them off to Willow and Jack.

We continued to laugh, and then the taunting escalated.

"How dare you!" I said, a glint in my eye.

Jack and Willow were excited. I had been winning, and now they saw their chance!

But then instead of continuing to grieve the loss of my letters and my spectacular words, something shifted inside. I became determined in that moment to rebuild, better than before.

I began to take everything apart quickly, and within seconds I realized—oh my God! I had literally every letter in the alphabet in my hand. I had multiple vowels. I could literally make any word. And so, within five minutes, I had quickly created a whole new board with even better words!

I ended up winning the game.

You Can Win Too, on Your Terms, If You Can Just Let Go of the Attachment to What You Think Winning Is Supposed to Look Like

When you are willing to pull some pieces apart and change something here and move some things around, you might realize that it's not as hard as you think to rebuild better than ever before. And, in fact, you might actually have fun doing it!

After playing for a little while longer, we realized that once you start throwing bombs at your own board, you play a lot better, have more fun, and win quickly. Before we know it, we were all picking new tiles instead of trying to force them into the existing words. We took apart words at every opportunity and formed new ones. By the end of the game, we were doing everything we could to rip everything apart again and again. The joy became exploring and creating something new. Rather than complaining about the letters we didn't get, and the letters we did get like those pesky Zs and Xs, we had all surrendered to the freedom that comes from loosening attachments.

This board game was a metaphor. I thought because I had been playing *Scrabble* for years that the way to play is to take what you get and make it work. But once circumstance forced me to question an assumption I have held since childhood, that's when the fun began. Lesson learned. I will always live a life of design, even if everyone else thinks that you get what you get and you try not to get upset, or you wait. And wait and wait.

Throughout the writing of this book, I wondered where my story might officially end. Where would we live? What would happen in my marriage? What might my business look like?

When people ask how I ended up here in this Colorado mountain town, I can point to this book. This is what Radical Living looks like in real time. I sold this book in late November, just a few weeks after Jeremy and I left Maine and headed to Florida. Later, after visiting dear friends and having a Thanksgiving meal I managed to cook with the small appliances I had bought in the RV, we sat at the kitchen table inside Andi while swarms of invisible insects called Ceratopogonidae, or "no-see-ums," lurked just outside the door. It was time to assess and adjust. One thing became very clear. In order to truly advance the Experiments we had undertaken during our year on the road—which were to assess what blows our hair back, explore where we might want to live, define what kind of lifestyle we wanted, and understand whether it would be possible to heal the pieces of our marriage that were broken—living in an RV full-time was not what we wanted anymore.

Instead, we wanted to explore slow travel in some of the top locations we were considering living in, as now we had new criteria. And we wanted to do it without being confined to living in a campsite. Most importantly, though, I knew it was time for me to take responsibility for considering what I really wanted in my life now, without being only concerned for what might make my husband happy. I needed to set some difficult boundaries with him. And follow through on them. I needed the space and time to write this book. And I also needed to reassess what I wanted my business to look like as I knew the Essence of what I do as a coach had less to do with dating and all to do with the work that is contained in these pages.

In short, we needed to rebuild through a different set of Experiments. And clearly, the Radical Living Challenge would always continue in some way. It was not, as I had thought, simply a one-year Experiment of living full time in an RV. This way of being and thinking had become a way of life. A way of constantly leaning in to the Seven Questions and through that continuing to experiment and grow more deeply into what and who I am. And inside that fluidity, Jeremy would be the husband I needed him to be, or he would not. But finally, it was clear to me, and to him. We had surfaced the new Essential Problem, and I had found myself inside another Newfound Gap.

All that said, Radical Living is unequivocally the absolute best challenge I have taken on. The net result is that for the first time in my life, I feel like each day is one I am creating.

I love waking up in the morning and seeing the new view. Not only the one I have from my deck, but also the new view I have of my inner and outer life. I love that I am becoming more of what I am, really, and I like this process and way of living very much. And best of all, I can now recognize in an instant when I am putting the needs of others in front of mine. How it impacts so much of what I do. Living the old way was a very well-developed muscle, and in recognizing it, now I can detach from it most of the time, and inside that spaciousness, I breathe. I get to make new choices. I can more easily reconnect to the other parts of me that are strong too. The badass, capable, playful, fun, and very-full-of-wonder parts of me. In fact, I love all the parts of me and relish that it is in fact, all of me that makes me, me. Of course, there are the external things that I am relishing too. I occasionally see horses in my backyard here. I have tried mountain biking. I started swimming during the summer, and even found myself on skis again. The feeling of stillness on the mountain made me giddy. That blew my hair back.

This morning, I stopped at an independent bookstore in my little mountain town. I have visited it almost weekly since we landed here to browse or grab a coffee. And every time I pause near the shelves where I know this book will live, I think about you, dear reader, and how I believe in you and your biggest dreams. Before you picked up this book, perhaps like me, you too were afraid of the bombs that inevitably get thrown at your life. But now you have been given the tools and the ability to live life by design rather than by default. Whether the bombs get thrown by circumstance or you set them off yourself, the Seven Questions and the framework of Life Design have activated the magic and the wisdom and the brilliance inside you. And with that power, imagine what you can do when you are living courageously, understanding that when we are brave, we set off a chain reaction that initiates the spark of joy and meaning.

Maybe you came into the process looking for a set of answers and were looking for spiritual guidance or even a way to get through something in your life that is difficult. And so instead of waiting for life to begin when your kids leave the nest, when you retire, when you are healed from your divorce, when you have a partner, or whatever you have set as the perfect time to begin living life on your terms, I remind you to seize the day now. You are able to make what is possible real. Create a life you love *now*. Ignite the spark. Take action on one question at a time. That's all that Radical Living is—a simple system that allows you to become more of what you are each day, allowing you to enjoy the journey as well as the destination. All you must do is follow it. You don't have to change or "fix" who you are for this to work. It just does.

Take one step in the Life Design Process today. See how fun it can be when you are able to stop worrying about the "what-ifs" and the metaphorical bombs of what might look to an outsider as a failure! And soon you will find that just as the sun sets and the sun rises and you are gifted with another day of life, the cumulative impact of your actions and courage will have yielded fruit. The kind of life and success that feels like a "hell yes," a life lived on your terms. And regardless of whether you win the day, get the guy, make the sale, or do whatever you used to do in order to feel satiated and full, you will know you have lived a full and meaningful life. Unintimidated by the messiness of it ever again. Simply put your Essential Self first, and everything else will fall into line. It's not rocket science, and you don't have to have to be ready to get it. Just try.

This is Radical Living.

WISDOM-SEEKING-QUESTIONS APPENDIX

The following questions are to support you in diving deeper into the concepts in this book. Some questions invite you to go on a 10-minute meditation walk with a question in mind and journal afterward. Others are simply journaling questions you can use at any time you feel stuck and want to access your wisdom. You can do them in any order.

What Is Your Essence?

- What are you becoming conscious of in this moment? (thoughts/feelings/sensations/other)

- What Essence qualities of yourself are you noticing, and what do each of these qualities mean to you?

- Beyond what you've just noticed, what other Essence qualities are coming into your consciousness now?

- Which areas of your life are most in alignment with, in resonance with, your Essence?

- In which areas of your life are you noticing dissonance for your Essence?

- What areas of deeper struggle are you noticing? What does your soul want for you here?

WALKING MEDITATION: Using a Wisdom-Seeking Question, choose one Essence quality to focus on what you discovered in Chapter 8. Then, set your intention to open to the physical sensation of this Essence. Set your timer for a 10-minute walk. As you walk, slow your pace down so your breath is gentle and rhythmic. During your walk, your mind will be organically receiving information from the environment, and your practice is to keep coming back to the sensations of the Essence quality and these questions:

- How does it feel to move with this quality?

- Where does the energy of this quality emanate from?

- How does it feel to be this quality?

  - Describe the sensations and physical qualities you noticed or are still noticing.

  - What was it like to move—to walk—with this Essence quality? What meaning does this have for you?

  - Free-write (stream of consciousness) as you reflect on your walk and all that you noticed around your sensations and your Essence.

  - In order to be fully expanded in your Essence, what will you want to/need to give up or let go of?

  - If you were living from this expanded place in your body, your being, how could your life be positively different than it is already?

  - To expand into your Essence even more, what will you need to truly believe?

How Deep Can You Go?

- What helps you to really tune in and listen to the wisdom of your Essential Self?

- When you are in the energy of listening to your inner being, what happens in your mind, emotions, body, and spirit/Essential Self?

- When you receive wisdom in your body, where do you feel it, and what are the surrounding circumstances and environment?

- What helps you to listen with others? (Get curious about your mind, emotions, and body.)

- What contributes to the shutting down of your knowing?

- What are some of the choices available to you instead of closing your energy down?

WALKING MEDITATION: Set your timer for a 10-minute walk. Keep your walking pace down so your breath is gentle and rhythmic. During your walk, remain open to information from the environment. While you walk, be in curiosity around these two questions:

- How does listening help create the life you love?

- How could you expand more into listening to your wisdom?

  - What did you discover around listening and wisdom?

  - How does courage help connect you to your wisdom?

  - Free-write (stream of consciousness) as you reflect upon your meditation walk and all that you noticed around your sensations, your thoughts, and your energy.

  - What does power mean to you? What associations do you have with being courageous or needing to be courageous?

- What is the effect on your capacity to be courageous when you feel loved and connected to others?

- What happens to your capacity to be courageous when you feel connected to your Essential Self and all the versions of you that have ever existed?

What Is the Pleasure of Now?

- What does it feel like in your body to become present?

- What is the effect of that presence on your nervous system and emotions?

WALKING MEDITATION: Set your timer for a 10-minute walk. While you walk, maintain a state of curiosity around these two questions:

- Which of your specific Essence qualities would have more expression when you're accessing presence?

- In your life relationships, how does presence connect to love and feeling loved?

  - How does trust relate to presence for you?

  - How does this relationship of trust and presence play out in your life?

  - If you were fully present in your everyday life, how would your life be different in your relationships with others? In your relationship with yourself?

  - How do you feel toward your mind? What's underneath those feelings?

  - How do you feel toward your emotional self? What's underneath those feelings?

- How do you feel toward your body? What's underneath those feelings?

- How do you feel toward your authentic Essential Self?

- Is there anything that needs healing in this moment? Breathe, be present to these aspects, and journal as you focus on an intention to heal.

What Will You Need to Do to Access True Power?

- How do you experience the feeling of home inside yourself?

- What might you want to let go of in order to trust the Universe more?

- How could surrendering to something greater than "you" increase your capacity for love? Your capacity to be? Your capacity to create?

- Which parts of not-you do you get to release when you are in radical faith?

- How does this strengthen you?

- How does this connect to your Essence and who you are becoming?

WALKING MEDITATION: Set your timer for a 10-minute walk. While you walk, be in curiosity around these two questions:

- How does radical faith support you in creating the life you love?

- How might you know when it is time to surrender?

  - What did you discover around surrender and power?

- What did you discover around surrender and trust?

- How do these discoveries connect to the tapestry of your life?

- Free-write (stream of consciousness) as you reflect on your walk and all that you are noticing now in your energy and your being.

- How is feeling grateful part of connection?

- How might connection support you to release what is no longer needed?

- What is soft about you right now? What beliefs could you release right now in this moment?

What Will You Need to Release to Feel Freedom?

- What did you notice in your body that supports you in freedom?

- What is the relationship between freedom and control?

- Are your current commitments supporting your freedom or holding it back?

Begin by selecting three life areas from the below list for your reflection. Then, set your timer and journal on the questions, for 10 minutes each question.

- Relationships—intimate/loved ones

- Relationships—professional

- Relationships—strangers

- Relationships—difficult/challenging ones

- Money

- Career/business

- Health
- Spirituality/religion
- Entertainment/enjoyment
- Any others

  - In what ways do you move away from freedom in this area of life?
  - What are some ways you could move toward freedom in these areas?
  - What are the "knots" of entanglement keeping you from accessing freedom or hindering your choices?

Consider knots of:

- Past drama/story
- Obligation
- Guilt
- Shame
- People-pleasing

- Fear
- Proving
- Resignation
- Any others

What Would Radical Faith Look Like for You?

Ask yourself:

- When I am triggered, what am I not having faith in?
- What are the ways I have cut myself off from faith?
- Where do I place my focus when I am in alignment with radical faith and my divine self?
- How does having radical faith create resilience in me?
- How do faith and compassion connect? How do they support my Essence?

- What is the problem in the way of my having radical faith?
- What is the problem in the way of my having self-compassion?
- Are there parts of me that I need to connect with to be in faith? How can I do that?

WALKING MEDITATION: Set your timer for a 10-minute walk. While you walk, be in curiosity around these two questions (either on the same walk, or use one question per walk):

- If I have radical faith in my Essential self, what else is possible?
- What else do I need to support my journey in accessing radical faith?
  - When I am being radical in faith, how do I bow to courage?
  - When I am being radical in faith, how do I bow to fear?
  - When I am being radical in faith, how do I bow to all parts of me?
  - What else do I need to support my journey in accessing radical faith?
  - How does radical faith support me in accessing compassion for others?
  - What can I release in order to choose compassion?
  - What does my Essential Self need from me to be radical in faith?

How Can You More Deeply Express Creation and Wonder?

If there is a current area in which you are feeling entangled, triggered, or blocked, use this situation as the basis for your journaling. For example, if you are triggered by a boss/partner/family member, you would apply "what are you intentionally creating" to that situation. Otherwise, you can approach the meditation and journaling with an open mind.

- What are you intentionally creating?

- If you could see the real higher truth of what you are creating, what would that mean for you in how you show up in the world?

- How might you take your interpretations of what you are creating and open even more to another perspective?

- What will you create that is lasting, that thing that will ripple through time and nurture those who come next?

- What will you need to leave behind in order to create that thing that is lasting and ripples through time?

- Are you living life in a way in which all time is precious and valuable? If you are in wonder, how could that help you connect to a sense of timelessness or time abundance?

WALKING MEDITATION: Set your timer for a 10-minute walk. While you walk, be in curiosity around these questions:

- What are you not aware of that you need to be aware of in order to create the life you're envisioning for yourself and for others you care about?

- What did you become aware of related to creating the life you envision for yourself and others?

- How are you wondering, and in which areas of your life?

- Where could you expand your sense of wonder, and how would that impact your creation?

- If you were truly designing and living your one precious and meaningful life, what would be different?

- What are the blessings around you that you are recognizing?

- Might you find blessings in chaos? How can the principle of creation and the skill of wonder allow you to access your wisdom?

- What other blessings are there that you could be recognizing that can help you have a breakthrough in an area in which you are entangled or blocked?

- How might recognizing more blessings elevate your ability to create?

What If You Allowed Yourself to Fully Choose Joy, without Conditions?

- What thoughts connect you to the felt sense of joy? Where do you feel an inner state of joy in your body? What does the sensation feel like? Describe it with your words. What else is present with the joy? What nuances, other feelings, emotions, energies, and states of being are there?

- Consider the emotions of frustrations, anger, resentment, powerlessness, and worry, and how they knot you. How might you replace these knots and dissonances with aliveness and joy?

- When you are in joy, what do you notice that is contained within a particular moment? What else do you notice within that moment? What else?

- If you were truly free to choose joy unconditionally, what would be different about you?

Pay attention to that ever-subtle, still voice inside, allowing it to emerge and speak more clearly. Breathe deeply and connect to those qualities, feelings, and states of joy.

From this space (be as specific as you can be), what are your beliefs about:

- your potential?

- your expectations?

- your "failures"?

- your work or purpose?

- your family?

    - Now, why do you believe these things about your potential, expectations, "failures," work/purpose, and family?

    - How do you know that you truly believe these things?

    - Which beliefs might be more how you want to be than how you are presently?

    - If you took direction from joy, how would it guide you? Who would/could you be and what would you do?

WALKING MEDITATION: First, set your timer for a 10-minute walk. Second, prepare for your walking meditation by breathing with your hand on your heart and "welcoming in joy" for one or two minutes. Feel into joy as you consider the following:

- Reflect on being and expressing joy and the beliefs you hold when you are connected to joy.

- How do you know that you truly believe these things?

- Which beliefs might be more how you want to be than how you are presently?

  - What have you been unaware of that you need to be aware of in order to bring joy and aliveness to all your days?

  - Where are you pretending to have joy, and what has kept you from raising your capacity for joy and being in full expression of it?

  - For any/all of the beliefs AND qualities of joy, how do you enact them? (Meaning how do you infuse yourself—through rituals, practices, exercises, thoughts, mantras, etc.—with these beliefs so that your actions, responses, perceptions all come from this place of belief and qualities of joy?)

  - What will you choose to leave behind so your capacity for joy reaches new heights?

  - What are the ego-based goals, achievements, wants, perfectionism, and addictions through which you have been trying to create joy and aliveness?

  - What are you ready to release to access a deeper level of joy or that which we call bliss?

What Will You Need to Do to Embody Your Soul?

- What are the feelings and sensations that you experience when you are embodied and centered? Remember to scan for the strongest sensations in your body and notice the subtle ones. As you write, continue to feel into the sensations that resonate with your true and authentic self.

- If you were to increase your familiarity with this state of beingness, how might your life become more synchronous, more easeful?

- What is something you now want to change in your life? How might it be easier to make that change when you are centered in this place of resonance?

- What opportunities might open up to you? What opportunities would you like to open up to you?

- What level of freedom would you like to reach in your being, and what is your commitment to having that level of freedom?

- What are some "building blocks" to embody Essential Self living?

- What consistent actions will you take that will stretch you into greater and greater alignment with your Essential Self?

- How are courage and action present in your life? Where are courage and action missing or lacking?

WALKING MEDITATION: Set your timer for a 10-minute walk. While you walk, be in curiosity around these two questions:

- How does being centered and embodied help you create the life you love?

- How does being embodied free your Essence and soul?

  - What is the relationship of unconditional safety to being embodied and to being free?

  - When you know you're unconditionally safe, what changes?

  - What shows up more that may be held back at other times?

  - If you were to know in your being that you are unconditionally safe as an embodied soul, what would change for you? How would your actions/inactions be different?

  - In what ways does stability support you in freedom?

  - In what ways does simplicity connect you to freedom?

  - Write a short story (a few paragraphs) about your Essence—your soul—being fully free and fully embodied within this life. What is your soul's experience?

  - What is a consistent action that will support you in the full expression of your Essence and soul? Remember that it's important to keep expanding through action, and not just actions that are comfortable.

ACKNOWLEDGMENTS

While writing this book I had the pleasure of teaching and coaching this process to dozens of clients who enthusiastically committed to the idea of living a designed life. Among them, I wish to especially acknowledge the first students of my course Live Life on Your Terms, who enrolled in a yearlong journey with me to explore this topic. I also want to thank the women and one man who were my "test drivers" as a I refined the life design process in the final phase of writing this book. They asked amazing questions and shared their journeys with me during 1:1 coaching sessions and in a group setting. Each of these beings inspired me to follow my intuition, knowing this work needed to be made available in a larger way, while staying committed, even when there were obstacles along the way.

I remain grateful for the few clients who truly let me be their partner as together we worked through each part of their life design process. Particularly: Laura, who at 71 years old inspires me every day in her commitment to living a meaningful life in her pursuit of building a French community both in Los Angeles and in France. Then there is Sandra, who decided to bail on corporate life in her mid-50s as a result of developing the practice of radical honesty and listening to her Essential Self so she could fulfill the mission of her soul and retire early to take over her father's business so she could work by his side. And Nancy, who is retiring and moving to Portugal in just a few months. And Alexandra, who took back her power at work so that she could finally prioritize joy, her health, and her children, which meant breaking a generational pattern of feeling the need to prove her worth as a woman through professional success. She is living life on her terms. All these women did so without blowing up their existing lives.

Many thanks to my spiritual coach, Luke Iorio, who has been helping me discover my Essential Self for the past 15 years. His mentoring has helped me live into the Seven Questions, allowing me to bring my mission to life through my work. Luke, who served as CEO at the Institute for Professional Excellence in Coaching (IPEC), helped me to blend the traditional coaching I learned there with the deep spiritual work and the Seven Questions concepts intrinsic to this book; he did this while encouraging me and insisting that I be brave. Without his coaching, difficult Wisdom-Seeking Questions, and quick responses to my endless requests for help on Voxer, I think I might have ended up as a puddle on the floor, especially during the death of my dad in 2019.

I also acknowledge the people and organizations from whom I have learned so much in my personal development since beginning the journey in 2006: the Hoffman Institute; teachers Ed McClune and Drew Horning; the staff at IPEC; Mat Boggs, Dr. Kerry Ann Rockquemore; and my first mentor in the genre of Life Design, Jess, co-founder of the Fioneers. I highly recommend "An Introduction to Design Thinking Process Guide," published by the Institute of Design at Stanford University. This basic introduction to the principles of Design Thinking were the launchpad for my application of this process to our lives as human beings.

Big thanks to the teachers and coaches who have helped me to become a writer and author. Sondy Daggett, my high school journalism teacher, at a time where I was desperately trying to find something I was good at, encouraged me to become a writer. Driving me from Cedar Rapids, Iowa, to journalism camp at Ball State University was above and beyond what most teachers will do for a student they believe in. Without her encouragement and mentorship, I would never have continued to pursue my love of writing.

After my divorce in 2004, I began taking writing classes again through the UCLA Extension program. In this community I met Samantha Dunn and Shawna Kenney. I want to thank Sam for being to me what she adeptly described herself as "a book therapist." She sat across from me at a table in the basement of her coffee-shop workshop in Orange County to help me begin the writing journey that ultimately became this book.

A simple thank-you doesn't feel enough to convey my love and appreciation for Shawna Kenney, my book muse and writing coach, who read every single draft of this book over the last three years. Her notes, encouragement, and love spurred me on daily. Without her partnership and weekly deadlines, I wouldn't have been able to share this gift with the world.

Thanks also to Pam Houston for admitting me into her DRAFT Program, which introduced me to the incredible writing teacher and author, Josh Mohr. Josh helped me turn the idea I had about Radical Living into the story structure and format you see in this book today. His talent as a developmental editor and teacher is unparalleled. I am grateful to have been his student for so long. I also want to acknowledge Mark Malatesta, who not only helped me find an agent for this book, but helped me uncover the power the Seven Questions could have as a framework for my work, after I first heard them in a sermon given by Rabbi Joel Nickerson at Wilshire Boulevard Temple in Los Angeles.

And finally, I thank my agent, Steven Harris, at CSG Literary Partners, who e-mailed me just minutes after I sent my query letter to him. Steve jumped on a Zoom call with me immediately to express his desire to put this work out into the world. When he said his community of authors were like family to him, and I saw that one of his other clients had said he helped to make her dream come true, I knew he was my person. Steve has been a champion for this book; and I am forever grateful for his support.

I want to also thank my incredible intern Makenna Gaeta who tirelessly helped me attend to the details of writing, especially in putting together the Wisdom-Seeking Questions you will find at the end of the book.

Finally, a huge thank-you to my editors: Melody Guy, for the passion she shared with me on this topic, and Sally Mason-Swaab, for seeing my vision through to an incredible end product. I feel tremendously blessed to have followed the writing breadcrumbs (for the last 20 years) that put each one of these incredible humans in my life for this book to come to fruition.

I wrote the first pages of this book in Australia, surrounded by my international family. And today, as I write these acknowledgments, I am sitting in their kitchen this time in rural France, amidst a box of tomatoes, books, and water bottles, surrounded by their love and support while they fry up scrambled eggs and bacon. And the smell of croissants is calling me! Thank you to my in-laws, Eric and Linda, who have made me their daughter over the last 15 years. It turns out they have also been an inspiration to me and Jeremy, showing us what it looks like to live a Radical Life. As young Brits in the 1960s they took off to live in South Africa, then, when my father-in-law wanted to escape the grind of his long commutes from the suburbs of England to London that took him away from his family, they emigrated to Singapore in the 1980s. Later they lived on a sailboat for seven years, traveling through Malaysia and Thailand. Today they live in France as vibrantly in their 80s as I imagine they always have. I tell my own children, "I want to be them when I grow up."

I remain deeply thankful to my parents, Rene and Don Ohsman, who raised me to travel, explore, and pursue all my dreams, sending me off happily to a ski program one winter in France when I was 10 years old, allowing me to return to Iowa both fluent in French and as an avid skier. That still blows me away. My parents were my first examples of how to turn nothing into something, and they have been guiding me through this journey in ways I cannot describe. I no longer need them to be proud of me, per se, but I know that what they would be most proud of is not that I achieved a goal, but that I keep creating and planting seeds.

I must also thank my cousin Kathy Hoffman, who is more like a sister to me. She is president of my fan club and her belief in me since I was a child helped me keep going amidst the thousands of rejections and hurdles along the way. She always takes my call. Except, of course, when she is playing pickleball.

Thank you to my three daughters: Kloey, Rayna, and Willow. You have always been my "why." And what I am most proud of is that I raised you to live a life according to what I have taught in this book. For you it is like breathing, and that means more to me than anything. While the stories here do not call out Kloey directly, she taught me so much about Design Thinking as a senior design consultant at Deloitte, which inspired the entire process I created in the Live Life on Your Terms course. I thank her for the hours she spent pouring over frameworks, for explaining all the PDFs with unlimited patience, and for working with my clients directly in class, teaching them how to discover the Essential Problem. This partnership has been priceless. She is a badass boss babe and an innovator; and working with her on this project as well as our work together to help young women in Africa has been a highlight of my life. I am forever grateful.

And finally, thank you to my husband, Jeremy. You have challenged me in so many ways; and for every single part of our beautiful life together, I am grateful. Without your commitment to living a Radical Life and urging me to dig deeper, I am not sure I would have ever uncovered my fears or been able to become more of who I really am. We have lived a blessed life because you curate it to be that way every single day. You are "Funcle Jeremy" to everyone for a reason, bringing fun and cool to the lives of many. Getting to design life with you is a blessing. Thank you for all the tech support and making sure I always had Internet and coffee every step of the way; for schlepping the Peloton around the country and setting it up in dozens of places, without much complaint; and for letting me write about you even when sometimes it's not pretty. And most of all, for giving me the space and encouragement to pursue all my dreams. I hope now that this book is written I have a little more time to sit on the couch and binge-watch reality TV shows next to you and give you a hard time about eating so much chocolate. I love you very much.

ABOUT THE AUTHOR

MARNI BATTISTA is an entrepreneur, author, transformational coach, podcast host, and radical truth seeker. Her straight-to-the-point podcast and page-turning books drop beautiful pearls of wisdom that will not only make you laugh but also provide life-changing stories of triumph and courage to stop letting life live you, and start *living* a life that's beyond your wildest dreams. Battista's works have appeared in the *LA Times* and *The New Yorker,* and she has made appearances on *Dr. Phil, On Air with Ryan Seacrest,* and the *Home & Family* TV show. Website: **MarniBattista.com**

Hay House Titles of Related Interest

YOU CAN HEAL YOUR LIFE, the movie,
starring Louise Hay & Friends
(available as an online streaming video)
www.hayhouse.com/louise-movie

THE SHIFT, the movie,
starring Dr. Wayne W. Dyer
(available as an online streaming video)
www.hayhouse.com/the-shift-movie

• • •

THE AWAKENED WAY: Making the Shift to a Divinely Guided Life, by
Suzanne Geisemann

*CHANGE YOUR QUESTIONS, CHANGE YOUR FUTURE: Overcome
Challenges and Create a New Vision for Your Life Using the Principles of
Solution Focused Brief Therapy,* by Elliott E. Connie and Adam S. Froerer

*INTENTIONALITY: A Groundbreaking Guide to Breath, Consciousness, and
Radical Self-Transformation,* by Finnian Kelly

*LIVE THE LIFE YOU DESERVE: How to Let Go of What No Longer Serves You
and Embody Your Highest Self,* by Sylvester McNutt III

*SPIRITUAL ACTIVATOR: 5 Steps to Clearing, Unblocking, and Protecting Your
Energy to Attract More Love, Joy, and Purpose,* by Oliver Niño

All of the above are available at your local bookstore,
or may be ordered by contacting Hay House (see next page).

• • •

We hope you enjoyed this Hay House book. If you'd like to receive our online catalog featuring additional information on Hay House books and products, or if you'd like to find out more about the Hay Foundation, please contact:

Hay House LLC, P.O. Box 5100, Carlsbad, CA 92018-5100
(760) 431-7695 or (800) 654-5126
www.hayhouse.com® • www.hayfoundation.org

———

Published in Australia by:
Hay House Australia Publishing Pty Ltd
18/36 Ralph St., Alexandria NSW 2015
Phone: +61 (02) 9669 4299
www.hayhouse.com.au

Published in the United Kingdom by:
Hay House UK Ltd
1st Floor, Crawford Corner,
91–93 Baker Street, London W1U 6QQ
Phone: +44 (0)20 3927 7290
www.hayhouse.co.uk

Published in India by:
Hay House Publishers (India) Pvt Ltd
Muskaan Complex, Plot No. 3,
B-2, Vasant Kunj, New Delhi 110 070
Phone: +91 11 41761620
www.hayhouse.co.in

———

Let Your Soul Grow

Experience life-changing transformation—one video at a time—with guidance from the world's leading experts.

www.healyourlifeplus.com

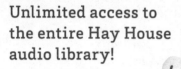